THE POLITICS OF
NOSTALGIA

In The Politics of Nostalgia, *Winlow takes us out
onto the streets of our forgotten towns and cities to
reveal lives destabilised by economic insecurity and
high-paced cultural change. In these places, nostalgia
is reshaping the political views of ordinary people,
but not in the ways we tend to assume. This is a
daring analysis of a nation tumbling downwards, a
nation in which more and more people see only dark
days ahead. . .* The Politics of Nostalgia *runs contrary
to so much mainstream analysis of contemporary
Britain, and it will be awkward reading for many
who would prefer to look away from the reality of
our nation today. Nonetheless, it offers an essential
examination of where we are now, and where we
appear to be going. . . It's also a reminder that a
much better Britain existed in the near past, and,
with sufficient public investment, a better future is
possible. Having given away our resources and past
to those with no interest in Britain, the state needs to
get us our resources in order to give us back our
future.*

—**Matthew Johnson, Professor of Public Policy and
Chair of the Common Sense Policy Group**

*This is an outstanding ethnographic study of a
crucial social and political issue. For the first time in
living memory, huge numbers of people believe the
future will be qualitatively worse than the present.
The data is sad but revelatory. Winlow's analysis is
full of pathos and insight, with occasional bursts of
anger at the refusal of our political elites to cast off*

the shackles of neoliberalism and reassert our commitment to the common good... Utterly compelling reading!

—James Treadwell, **Professor of Criminology, Staffordshire University**

The Politics of Nostalgia *is a boundary-redefining ethnographic analysis of the rootlessness and decline overwhelming Britain today. In focusing on the sentiments of those who feel increasingly lost in today's fast-paced society, and their nostalgic attachment to a world that once made sense, Simon Winlow offers a crucial understanding of our current political conjuncture. Essential reading.*

—Anthony Lloyd, **Professor of Sociology, Teesside University**

Simon Winlow has long been the outstanding criminologist working in Britain and The Politics of Nostalgia *enhances his already stellar reputation. Beautifully written and sensitively researched, it returns to one of his enduring themes – how class remains the best means of illuminating what is hidden in contemporary British society and why looking back provides solace, reassurance and a powerful sense of self-narration.*

—David Wilson, Emeritus Professor of Criminology, Birmingham City University

THE POLITICS OF NOSTALGIA

Class, Rootlessness and Decline

BY

SIMON WINLOW
Northumbria University, UK

emerald
PUBLISHING

United Kingdom – North America – Japan – India
Malaysia – China

Emerald Publishing Limited
Emerald Publishing, Floor 5, Northspring, 21-23 Wellington Street,
Leeds LS1 4DL

First edition 2025

Reprints and permissions service
Contact: www.copyright.com

British Library Cataloguing in Publication Data
A catalogue record for this book is available from the British Library

ISBN: 978-1-83753-551-4 (Print)
ISBN: 978-1-83753-548-4 (Online)
ISBN: 978-1-83753-550-7 (Epub)

CONTENTS

About the Author   *ix*

Acknowledgements   *xi*

Introduction: Falling   1
1. The New Politics of Nostalgia   29
2. Fearing the Future   61
3. Lost Roots   79
4. Beyond Modernism   95
5. Permanent Reform   115
6. Intimations of Post-Sociality   141
7. Towards a Better Future   153

Endnotes   *163*

Bibliography   *177*

ABOUT THE AUTHOR

Simon Winlow is a Professor of Social Science at Northumbria University, UK. He is the author or coauthor of the following books: *Badfellas: Crime, Tradition and New Masculinities* (Berg, 2001); *Bouncers: Violence and Governance in the Night-time Economy* (Oxford University Press, 2003) *Violent Night: Urban Leisure and Contemporary Culture* (Berg, 2004) *Criminal Identities and Consumer Culture: Crime, Exclusion and the New Culture of Narcissism* (Willan, 2008); *Rethinking Social Exclusion: The Death of the Social?* (Sage, 2012); *Riots and Political Protest: Notes from the Post-Political Present* (Routledge, 2015); *Revitalizing Criminological Theory: Towards a New Ultra-Realism* (Routledge, 2015); *Rise of the Right: English Nationalism and the Transformation of Working-Class Politics* (Policy, 2017), and *Death of the Left: Why we must begin from the beginning again* (Policy, 2022).

ACKNOWLEDGEMENTS

The book you are holding in your hands offers a brief glimpse into what was a large longitudinal ethnographic study investigating the evolving political views of a sample of ordinary people living somewhere in the north of England. These men and women generously gave up their time to talk to me about their lives, and for that, I will be forever grateful. I would especially like to thank the characters I call Arthur and Paul for giving me so much help tracking down people who had illuminating things to say about nostalgia, culture, politics and change. I am also very grateful to The Leverhulme Trust, who funded this research project. To be given two years to pursue research of this kind is incredibly rare, and I am very thankful to the Trust for its generosity.

I must also thank a large number of academic colleagues who have assisted me in one way or another. First, I must thank Steve Hall and Tom Raymen for kindly reading through and commenting on the first draft of this book. Their insights certainly helped me to tighten my analysis and improve the overall quality of this book. I should also thank my colleagues Dan Briggs, Justin Kotze, Alex Hall, Georgios Antonopoulos, Matthew Johnson, Sarah Soppitt, Nick Gibbs and Mark Bushell, all of whom work hard every day to ensure that intellectual matters remain a key feature of our day-to-day working lives. To that list, I should add the names of a range of academics who also embody all that remains good in inquisitive, objective social science: Anthony Lloyd, James Treadwell, Tammy Ayres, Pat Carlen, Tony Ellis, David Wilson, Dick Hobbs, Keith Hayward, Walter DeKeseredy, Luke Telford, Kate Tudor, Robert Reiner, Lisa McKenzie, Adam Lynes, Deirdre O'Neill, Elissavet Farmaki, Rowland Atkinson, Grace Gallagher, Craig Kelly, Emma Armstrong, Lee Jones, Paul Alker, Parisa Diba, Sam Barnes, David Temple, Owen Hodgkinson, Elaine Campbell, Peter Squires, Dan Rusu, Liam Brolan, Tereza Østbø Kuldova, Alex Hochuli, Phil Cunliffe and George Hoare.

I must also take this opportunity to extend my love and gratitude to my extended family. However, I reserve special praise for my beautiful wife, Emma, and my wonderful son, Gabriel. The Winlow clan were also, during the writing of this book, lucky enough to welcome a baby boy. Roman made his grand entrance on the 20 May 2024, and he has already added immeasurably to the joyfulness of our happy home.

INTRODUCTION: FALLING

Nostalgia seems to be everywhere these days. It clearly shapes a broad range of trends in consumer culture. We can see it in the movies and television shows we watch, in the products we buy and of course in the ubiquitous marketing messages that subtly shape our leisure habits. We can also identify the manipulation of its seductive appeal in the realm of politics and especially in the new populist movements that purport to threaten the dour political consensus that continues to bear down so heavily upon ordinary people.

In its original conception, the word 'nostalgia' was used to capture the discomfort of homesickness.[1] To be in the grip of nostalgia was to be plagued by powerful, sentimental memories and a deep yearning to again experience the various comforts we associate with home. Of course, both intellectuals and ordinary people have understood and used the concept of nostalgia in a variety of ways, and its core meaning has evolved slightly over time. Initially, I saw this book as a response to nostalgia's recent politicisation, a process that has stripped away many of nostalgia's traditional symbolic features before pressing a revised version of the concept into the service of robust political and cultural critique, much of it aimed at the working class, or at least the working class as it is perceived by the progressive neoliberals who now manage many of our core institutions.[2] My hope was to move beyond hostile, divisive and inaccurate cultural criticism to address honestly and accurately how, why and to what extent nostalgia informs the political attitudes of the British working class today. However, as my research developed, new themes emerged to carry my analysis in a slightly different direction.

The research project at the centre of this book took around two years to complete.[3] I used ethnographic research methods to investigate the lives and shifting political sensibilities of working-class voters in and around a post-industrial city in the north of England.[4] In total, I spoke to around 70 men and women, all of whom were between the ages of 45 and 60. Overwhelmingly, my participants came from what is commonly termed 'the traditional working class'. Most of the men worked in manual trades. They were builders, mechanics, plumbers, joiners, kitchen fitters, heating engineers, machine operators and factory workers. Some had passed through manual trades and ascended to lower managerial positions in the construction and manufacturing industries.

A smaller but still significant number of my contacts, both male and female, fitted quite neatly into what we might call 'the new working class'. They were call centre workers, retail workers, salespeople and administrators. Rather than working with their hands, they spent their days on the shop floor or behind a desk, talking to customers and carrying out various administrative tasks.[5] I also spoke to men and women who had moved between these two groups. In each instance, this involved a move from traditional working-class labour into newer occupations associated with the post-industrial working class. This shift from traditional to newer forms of working-class work is indicative of the deep changes that have taken place in our national and global economies.[6] As most readers will know, Britain's industrial sector shrank as neoliberalism established itself as a global orthodoxy during the 1980s.[7] Manufacturing moved to the east and to the developing world, where corporations could take advantage of low labour costs, low taxes, minimal regulation and the sparsity of trade unions. Consumerism grew, and in the wake of a prodigious decline in its manufacturing industries, Britain became reliant upon imported goods. As the neoliberal era developed, it became increasingly clear that many workers in Britain would need to look to the growing and diversifying service sector for the jobs they needed to sustain themselves.[8] However, most jobs available in this sector were poorly paid and insecure, and many more were short-term and non-unionised.

The social and cultural effects of deindustrialisation were huge.[9] In many respects, they act as a crucial contextual background for this study. In the broadest sense, the forms of security and rootedness that existed during the modern industrial era – in particular those that stemmed from the willingness of a succession of governments to intervene in the economy in an effort to ensure stability, safety and adequate standards of living – frame the nostalgic memories of my participants when they reflect upon what they have lost and where they are now. Similarly, the sense of impermanence and insecurity often associated with the post-industrial era finds expression when participants discuss their present difficulties and their fears for the future.

It is often said that the decline of modern British industrialism inevitably led to the decline of Britain's old industrial working class.[10] Britain's post-industrial economy spurred the growth of what seemed to be an entirely new working class, more diverse, mobile, urban and adaptable than the old.[11] There is certainly some truth to this. The forms of work that now seem to constitute 'working-class labour' vary enormously, and the cultural forms that characterised the working class during the modern era have either evolved at great speed or disappeared entirely. High levels of net immigration have made the working class much more diverse in terms of culture, ethnicity and religion. The working-class men and women who cluster in our largest cities can seem at first glance to have nothing at all in common with the standard stereotypes we associate with the old working class. Nor do they seem to have much in common with the predominantly white post-industrial working class that can still be found in huge numbers in regions once dominated by heavy industry. However, in our rush to embrace the new and cleave ourselves apart from the old we should not overlook the forms of continuity and commonality that can still be found below the surface diversity of everyday life.[12]

With regard to my research, there were no significant differences between manual and non-manual workers. They did not view the field of politics differently, and they tended to be nostalgic for similar times, experiences and objects. They lived in the same neighbourhoods and, broadly speaking, their leisure lives were composed of the same interests and pastimes. They also tended to express a similar range of anxieties about the future, and their complaints about the present tended to focus on the same fundamental issues. Their jobs were a little different, but both groups were working class. They occupied the same structural position in the socio-economic hierarchy, and they shared a common culture.

It is difficult to deny that working-class work is far more varied than it once was. Clearly, the working class are no longer clustered in a rather narrow band of productive, extractive and manufacturing industries. Nor can they be found teeming out of mines, shipyards and factories in quite the numbers they once did. However, while they may be slightly harder to spot, there can be little doubt that they continue to play a central role in our national economy. They can of course be found throughout our sprawling service sector and in what remains of the productive economy. They can also be found working in construction and throughout our agricultural and tourist industries. In line with this diversity, the incomes associated with working-class work now vary enormously. For some, work is so poorly paid that they remain very firmly 'in poverty'.[13] For others, working-class work pays enough to secure a standard of living we might once have associated with the lower reaches of the old middle class.[14]

While income disparities among the working-class have grown, they are certainly not new. Nor are discussions about whether, in the face of what often appears to be boundless diversity and change, it is worth persevering with 'the working class' as a cultural and socio-political category.[15] We can also casually throw into this bubbling cauldron of apparently incessant change the fact that, throughout the neoliberal era, middle-class work has also stretched, swelled and shifted, gradually encroaching upon terrain that once belonged solely to the old working class.[16] Many men and women with impressive qualifications, and some with stereotypically middle-class cultural characteristics, now find themselves in downgraded, insecure and 'proletarianised' jobs that grant few if any of the advantages once associated with middle-class employment. What remains to bond together the more affluent elements of the old middle class with those downgraded and insecure but credentialised men and women who find themselves locked into a perpetual struggle to make ends meet? Is the entire idea of social class now useless, a relic from a bygone age, a form of categorisation that no longer accurately captures and reflects the realities of a transformed Britain?

Such debates have raged on for decades, and often it seems that we have made little forward motion. It is certainly true that the cultural life of the people has undergone enormous change. It is also true that labour markets have been radically overhauled. Our economic lives are more precarious, and the ways we engage with the world of work have evolved a great deal in a relatively short period of time. The relationship between the employer and the employee has also shifted in ways that reflect underlying economic change. In Britain, the reasonably organic forms of culture that still existed in the latter half of the 20th century are now very difficult to identify. Our popular culture has been commercialised and dumbed down. The public realm has been stripped back and sold off. Growing numbers of people – anxious about the dangers of public space and keen to avoid awkward or unwanted encounters with others – increasingly want *off this world*.[17] Some want to float among their own high ideals, distant from the perceived decay of the real world and the grubbiness of social experience. Responding to the disintegration of 20th century liberalism, and the diffusion of what were once its constitutive fragments, some embrace atomisation and construct in their imagination appealing images of the sovereign self that might salve their prevailing sense of loss as we hurtle into an unknowable future.

In any case, it is difficult to deny the retreat to the private realm and the forms of mediated sociality that can be found there. Obvious examples of apparently vibrant sociality today often communicate an awkward sense of simulation and rarely exist independently of commercial imperatives. It seems unlikely that the collective identities of the modern age can be sustained much further into the 21st century.[18] Where they can be found they tend to be absent of the forms of belief that once gave them their vitality and significance. All of these things, and much else besides, linger in the background of debates about class. Can we construct an objective conception of class amid the tumult of a disintegrating social order?

To briefly simplify, those who offer essentially liberal accounts of changing Britain often suggest that the concept of social class has become old fashioned and unwieldy. It is now incapable of accurately capturing a fluid social order in which ordinary people have been liberated from the modern age's restrictive structures and protocols and can now creatively construct and reconstruct their identities as they see fit.

Traditional materialists and their fellow travellers on the other side of the argument continue to stress that social classes are the product of unjust economic arrangements. The observable cultural characteristics of class groups are complex and ephemeral creations that grow from a shared position within the formal economy. Changes to the structure of the social class system are predictable and routine and do not threaten the continuity of the system itself.

There is value to be found on both sides of the argument. It is certainly true that ordinary people no longer feel *enclassed* to anything like the extent they once did. While class was a key tool used by their parents and grandparents to understand themselves, their identities, their socio-economic status and their relation to others, young people today tend to draw on a broader range of cultural resources as they construct their self-images. And what is left of class if it is not felt? What is left if people no longer invest in it and use its logic and symbolism to make sense of themselves and their lives? Does class retain any positive political symbolism? Can it be simply bequeathed to social scientists, becoming solely a means of separating groups of people so that they might be targeted with more culturally appropriate corporate messaging? Readers will be aware that class now plays a much-reduced role in popular culture.[19] It has also been jettisoned from mainstream political debate. Even the Labour Party, which was formed to advance the interests of Britain's working class, refuses to use class as an instrument of social analysis or an anchor for policymaking.

The disappearance of class from the public sphere is one of many symptoms of our ongoing political malaise and the prohibition that has been placed upon policy innovation and the kinds of deep socio-economic interventions we need to address our most pressing problems. Rather than being simply a logical outcome of the rise of consumerism and the perceived growth of opportunities to make active decisions about who we are and what matters to us, it behoves us to fully investigate the possibility that class has been strategically withdrawn from political debate in order to disguise and repress the continuing reality of class antagonism.

The strategic withdrawal of class analysis has aided the broad and dispiriting popular acceptance that today's dominant form of political economy represents a historical end point, beyond which nothing positive might emerge.[20] The competition inherent to neoliberal capitalism's social order is, in the absence of class analysis, for the most part naturalised: rendered unproblematic and unavoidable. Rather than moving with others onto the field of politics in the hopes of fashioning something better, the sovereign individual must throw herself into the ceaseless battle of all against all to achieve a modicum of material comfort and security.

Large sections of the left have relieved themselves of the weight of traditional leftist accounts of class conflict as they have rushed to lend support to new identitarian struggles. Rather than pushing for the abandonment of competition, they tend to petition authority to make the competition fairer. The absence of serious thinking on the left about how our economies can be significantly reformed or revolutionised is one of the principal reasons why the left no longer represents a significant electoral force.[21] And yet the injustices of our present economic system are legion. The gap between rich and poor grows wider with every passing year, and the malignant effects of poverty and income inequality are everywhere to be seen.[22] The broad left's determined effort to foreground the struggles of marginalised identity groups unfortunately tends to overlook the fact that each identitarian group is organised hierarchically, with educated middle-class liberals taking a leading role and the material interests of the group's usually expansive working class largely forgotten.[23]

For two centuries across the west, a partially hidden ideological war has raged to rid individualism of the stain of ethical failure while fragmenting and de-politicising all traditional and incipient collective groups and identities. As time has worn on, a defending ragtag army of collectivists has found itself surrounded and besieged. This war has not quite drawn to a decisive conclusion, but there can be little doubt that the forces of individualism have had the upper hand for some time. The neoliberal era can be reasonably understood as a key theatre of conflict in this war on collectivism, its aspiration to atomise, commodify, de-politicise and control, to reconfigure all drives to transform the external world into the incessant drive to transform the self, to erode obligation and sacrifice and champion the endless proliferation and pursuit of stupid pleasures in the name of freedom.

Class remains a vital unifying concept for the left. Rather than accentuating differences, it draws cultural groups together by focusing upon those things that are shared. And despite the ongoing attempts to transform the left and equip it with updated intellectual weaponry, it is important to acknowledge that class politics remains the only force that has thus far been able to force significant modification upon the system. Solidarity and common cause have proven themselves capable of shifting the trajectory of history, while individualism and difference can be immediately accommodated by a self-revolutionising market system that welcomes all as individual competitors into its circuits of production, exchange, consumption and investment. We might reasonably interpret ongoing political attempts to negate the politics of class as a backhanded acknowledgement of the concept's latent power.

The broad left appears to have willingly disarmed itself. Rather than encouraging the people to acknowledge common interests and inspiring them with tales of solidarity's great power, large sections of the left have sauntered off in the opposite direction. The contemporary mainstream left in Britain is now overwhelmingly 'middle class'.[24] It has dispensed with its residual cultural conservatism and is now overwhelmingly 'liberal'. It's great commitment to cosmopolitanism has led it to chastise and ridicule those who remain emotionally invested in their locales and regions, even if those people might be otherwise committed to the traditional goals of the left. It has jettisoned true solidarity and now seems principally concerned with difference, diversity and the rights of the individual. Rather than break down barriers and encourage ordinary people to acknowledge common interests, its fundamental drive is towards separation and distinction. The left no longer sees itself as a power in waiting, and for the most part, it no longer proposes significant social and economic transformation. Instead, many strands of the left seem happy to transform themselves into an agglomeration of disparate activist movements, each of which hope to advance the interests of a specific micro-community within the system as it stands.

Rather than digress any further, I will simply note that I am firmly of the view that an updated analysis of class can illuminate much that is hidden in contemporary British society. While it probably goes without saying, I should also state clearly that this book is about the working class. It explores where the working classes are now. It attempts to give voice to their complex thoughts and feelings about the movement of history and their growing recognition of their own political and cultural irrelevance. It addresses, from a multiplicity of angles, their obdurate sense that the future is somehow not for them, and their clear conviction that their cultures, skills and political sensibilities have been quietly abandoned and left behind as Britain stumbles guilelessly forwards, unaware of the value of what has been discarded and apparently unconcerned about the dangers that lie ahead.

METHODS

Most research participants were white men. A significant minority described themselves as Christian, but most were atheists. No participants aligned themselves with any other religion. Mostly, I spoke to men and women who were in full-time employment. I spoke to a small number of men who were out of work and in receipt of state benefits. In each case, these men had been judged too sick to work. I did not talk to research participants about their sexual interests. Such matters didn't seem pertinent. Of course, participants often discussed past relationships, and we also spent a good deal of time discussing key life events, such as bereavement, marriage, divorce and becoming a parent. These discussions led me to the conclusion that most of the men and women I spoke to were heterosexual.

In important ways, research participants' surface characteristics reflected who I am and the practicalities of conducting this kind of research.[25] Ethnography – the research method I used to gather the data that appears in this book – can yield great detail.[26] I spent a lot of time simply chatting with research participants. We walked around their neighbourhoods. They showed me the houses they had grown up in. We looked at their old schools and former workplaces, at boarded up nightclubs and at apparently innocuous urban street corners where important events in their lives had unfolded. I gathered their stories and asked what seemed to me to be pertinent questions. I tried tentatively to steer our discussions to politics and change.

Initially, some participants struggled to cast their minds back to key events from their personal pasts. Remembering required effort. It was of course unusual for them to be asked to talk about their lives in detail. However, once into the swing of things, conversations could last for hours. The struggle to remember is actually quite important. Participants often seemed firmly lodged in a present time orientation and rarely thought much about the future or the past. They mobilised standard arguments about incessant busyness and feeling engulfed by a huge diversity of demands upon their time. They talked of being constantly assailed by the usual practicalities of everyday life, of perennial anxieties about work and their children and grandchildren and of course the fragility of their financial position. However, some admitted to spending too much time on social media. Figuratively chained to their phones, they watched videos sent to them, responded to a constant stream of messages and scrolled through acres of online content. Such activities required a degree of focus and yielded a very shallow measure of gratification. Some also admitted to spending hours shopping online, only to back away at the final hurdle to avoid completing the purchase. Such things seemed to crowd out opportunities to engage in the kinds of deep, ruminative thought that interested me.[27] It was common for participants to encounter questions about the future as if thinking about such matters for the first time. It was also common for participants to move slowly from vagueness to precision when outlining noteworthy memories. Such matters elongated our discussions, but it did so productively. The more we talked, the more I came to know and understand them. Slowly, over the course of the research project, a central thesis began to emerge. I then tested out ideas, retaining and refining some while abandoning others.

I adopted this strategy because I was interested not simply in basic facts or amassing huge reams of data that might be used to build a succession of academic publications. I was not particularly concerned with the size of my sample or its representativeness. The neighbourhoods I researched are still populated overwhelmingly by white members of the working class, and I spoke to as many people as I could.[28] Slowly, a smaller group of key research participants emerged. Occasionally, they expressed an interest in the topic and wanted to get involved. Sometimes, they simply found themselves with time on their hands and were happy to help me out. A smaller number were particularly animated about politics and saw engaging in the project as an opportunity to air their views.

I was of course interested in research participants' emotional responses to change. I wanted to get at the complexities of thought and feeling that are bound up with nostalgic memories, and I was lucky enough to have the time and space to explore these issues in great depth. Of course, such a task requires focus. To produce the kinds of data I wanted, it was necessary to work with quite a small sample of working-class men and women. In order to persuade ordinary people to talk in detail about their lives – to get them to dig down into half-forgotten memories and divulge and appraise the emotions that accompany such memories – it is necessary to build rapport. One can't just turn up with a clipboard and a list of questions and assume that everyone will be immediately willing to talk openly and honestly about their intimate personal histories or reveal their deepest thoughts about politics, change and the future.

I was lucky enough to call upon a range of personal contacts who have helped me with previous research projects. These men acted as guides and introduced me to others who might be willing to talk to me. I focused on places I knew quite well. My ability to conduct this kind of research effectively rested upon my ability to get to know research participants and to allow them to get to know me. I come from a working-class background, and I am around the same age as research participants. We share a common culture. I was immediately conversant with subtle codes of speech and conduct. I knew the history of the neighbourhoods where I conducted the research. I knew when to laugh and when to shut up. I knew when to push forwards and when to back off. Quite often, we had friends and acquaintances in common. More than once, I discovered that research participants and I had attended the same school. One participant remembered me from a pub I used to frequent. In research of this kind, initial conversations often begin with attempts to close down distances and find connections and common experiences so that more informal talk can begin. In the context of this research, my background was a huge advantage. It allowed me to move forward far more quickly than would have otherwise been the case.

I decided to interview mostly white members of the post-industrial working class because I was already embedded in their world. It was easier for me to talk to men because men more readily made themselves available to me for conversation. The men who helped me to identify potential participants also had a greater number of male contacts. I did not set out to interview men specifically, but given my experience in conducting this kind of research, it did not concern me that things tended to move organically in that direction.

If I had attempted to research, for example, Muslim women working in working-class service sector jobs, I would not have been able to capitalise on my own cultural heritage and identity, my prior knowledge of the researched culture or the presence of established research contacts within the culture itself. It would not be impossible for me to research such a group of women, but my chances of revealing and accurately appraising cultural complexities would diminish. In studies of this kind, it is best to try to steer participants beyond immediate and unthinking responses. The truly important stuff is often hidden or obscured and difficult to get at. However, as familiarity develops and participants begin to feel more comfortable, it becomes possible to encourage them to appraise their lives a little more thoughtfully. Encouraging participants to be reflective and contemplative and to feel free to say whatever they'd like without fear of condemnation or critique can produce revelatory data that can drag sterile academic debates onto more fertile intellectual ground.

If one hopes to produce data of this kind, it is a huge advantage to have a highly developed understanding of the researched culture. In many respects, if one is really committed to the forms of deep ethnographic analysis I have alluded to above, researching working-class Muslim women with jobs in the service sector is a job suited to a working-class Muslim woman. It is not that researchers from other backgrounds have nothing to contribute or stand little chance of success. Rather, it is that a researcher with a highly nuanced cultural understanding of the researched group stands a better chance of being able to identify hidden meanings and inferences, untangle complex forms of cultural shorthand and of course recognise and comply with the partially submerged rules that hold cultures together.

Inevitably, when discussing research of this kind, it is necessary to address the issues of representativeness and generalisability. In truth, I have little to add to what is an apparently interminable circular argument about the relative merits of qualitative research methodologies. Ethnographic studies of cultures in action inevitably focus on small numbers of people. This is not a survey. I have made no attempt to construct a dataset that reflects every unique point on the social spectrum. Instead, I see this study as a synecdoche: a small part of a much greater whole, but one that is nonetheless representative of that greater whole. While I have studied a relatively small number of mostly white working-class men and women from the north of England, I believe the themes used to give shape to their thoughts and feelings about politics and change are, at least in part, generalisable. I believe these forms of analysis have the capacity to shed light upon the emotional lives of every distinct cultural group that forms part of the contemporary British working class.[29]

While my analysis focuses in a very direct way upon the ex-industrial working class of northern England, the thoughts and feelings of participants reflect the changing structures and processes that pattern the lives of ordinary working people across Britain. They reflect the evolving economic and political fortunes of the working class in its entirety. While there are important nuances and variations, their anxieties about money and the future are broadly felt throughout our society. As we will see, their nagging sense of their own cultural and economic irrelevance is complex, but it is far from being unique to this specific cultural group. Similarly, the patterns that are to be found within their nostalgic memories are likely to be broadly similar to those found throughout the multi-ethnic working class. The challenges of ageing, and the emotions stirred by the growing recognition that one's best days are gone, are also broadly generalisable.

My research participants are towards the bottom of the income scale. They tend not to be the poorest. Almost all research participants held legitimate jobs of some kind. However, they all experienced significant financial pressures. For some, these pressures relate to meeting mortgage payments and safeguarding their children while attempting to maintain or recreate at least some semblance of a meaningful social life. For others, the pressures were more extreme. Simply attempting to meet their immediate material needs concentrated the mind to the extent that other considerations tended to fall by the wayside. Anxieties about the future, growing discomfort in the present and a general hankering for elements of the past ripple through the entire social body. These broad trends deserve critical interrogation. They should inspire ambitious policy innovations, but there are currently no signs that such policy innovations will emerge. It seems to me inevitable that, left quietly to atrophy in the background, these things will eventually inspire a return to politics that is unlikely to tally with our own ideological preferences.

As we will see, some research participants seem to have lived through very difficult times. Some suffer from rapidly declining health. A small number had effectively retired early and were in receipt of disability benefits. Others act as an informal carer for a family member. The pay of some was so meagre they received housing benefit. Stories of divorce, bereavement, and fractured relationships were common. Many were dissatisfied with their employment and not just because they believe themselves to be poorly paid for the work they do. Some were bored. Others felt over-worked, under-paid and over-burdened, exhausted by their employment but, for various reasons, unable to let it go. Again, these experiences are common throughout Britain's culturally variegated working class. These experiences bleed into the attitudes of research participants and subtly mould their interpretations of politics and change.

FACING DECLINE

I hope the book you are holding in your hands can act as a portal to a world far from the cultural mainstream. It is a short book and consequently absent of much of the contextual material one usually finds in ethnographic studies of cultures in action. While I have a huge stock of empirical data available to me, I offer few direct quotations. Instead, for the sake of brevity, I have attempted to describe the lives of research participants and what they had to say about politics, change and their own personal pasts. I talk in generalities about what many or most research participants think or feel. While in retrospect it would have been useful to have the space to include more description and detail, I am confident that I have accurately captured their predicament, and I have not strategically accentuated or revised any aspect of their views, attitudes or circumstances. My overall analysis, the tone of my critique and the various strands of theory I deploy seem to me to be the most appropriate, applicable and convincing, but here of course the reader is free to disagree. I am committed to honest empirical research, but if we are to better understand the times in which we live, it is also vital that we retain a space for speculative and creative analysis. In the pages ahead, we will look closely at what research participants are nostalgic for, and why particular images of the past have been judged retrospectively important. Ultimately, using empirical data as its foundation, this book attempts to build a new, accurate and objective account of precisely why contemporary working-class politics seems irrevocably tied to the past.

As we will see, it is no surprise that so many working-class men and women look back to their personal and shared histories to identify something positive. It is no surprise because it is now abundantly clear that the British working class are without worthwhile political representation.[30] It is no surprise because, for the British working class, standards of living have fallen precipitously, and nowhere on the field of politics is there any evidence that this long-running trend will soon be reversed.[31,32] It makes absolute sense for my contacts to be apprehensive about the future, just as it makes absolute sense for them to complain about the present. If you were in their position, you would no doubt feel the same. It is difficult for them to maintain a worldly sense of hope, but they can recall times when it was otherwise. It was not ever thus.

Now is a time of great instability and portent. Neoliberal globalism has dominated politics for decades, but it is now edging ignominiously towards its end.[33] Neoliberalism has been profoundly antisocial and rooted in often dehumanising, extreme and reckless exploitation. It reallocated power and resources from the social body to new elites that seem increasingly beyond both the law and the obligations that pertain to citizenship. It disempowered the state and placed the interests of oligarchs and investors beyond the remit of democratically elected governments. It also aided the decomposition of civil society and corroded many things of great value to ordinary people. However, despite these things, it is difficult to celebrate the end of neoliberal market capitalism because what is emerging in its wake seems to be significantly worse.

It's tough to remain attached to the conventional belief that the future will surpass the present, but many still cling to it by their fingernails because there is comfort to be found in convincing oneself that better days lie ahead. While it remains easy to get lost in daydreams about an idealised future, very often we are returned to a reality that suggests growing hardship, fragmentation, enmity and loss. Security may not be restored. Lost freedoms may not be reinstated. Simmering antagonisms may not cool. Perhaps the obscene freedoms of the super-rich will advance rather than recede. Perhaps the deconstruction of the modern welfare state will not be reversed and will instead pick up pace. Perhaps our children will not climb higher. Perhaps they will not live happier and more contented lives. Perhaps our troubles will be as nothing compared to the troubles our grandchildren and great grandchildren are destined to experience.

A sense of decline thus permeates this book. However, its exploration of decline is not rooted in mere pessimism. If we are to understand our present epoch, if we are to truly get a firm grip on where we are now and where we appear to be heading, we must ruthlessly jettison groundless emotivism and approach the real world with openness and honesty.[34] While so many commentators seem determined to flee the real world in search of the comforts of an ideologically constituted utopia, what we need more than ever is a dogged realism that will not yield ground despite being subject to constant salvos launched by the discomforted Rawlsian liberals who occupy the high ground in our institutions and throughout much of our culture.[35] We must commit ourselves to representing the real world as it is and forego the fashionable trend of representing it in ways that reflect our political commitments. Only when we are armed with a clear and objective account of our present problems will we possess the wherewithal to do anything about them.

In the interests of honesty, I should disclose that my research often revealed the opposite of what I hoped to find. It would've bolstered my spirits to find political commitment, organic resistance, and a desire to join with others to fight our way clear of neoliberalism's dismal climate of desperation, under investment and chronic insecurity. But that is not what I found. Many of my contacts saw dark days ahead. The dominant narratives they offered to me – as we spoke about politics and their lives, past and present – revolved around absence.[36] My contacts spoke of disintegrating social bonds, rising crime and conflict, increasingly overt and hard-edged cultural antagonisms, worsening forms of material hardship and the withering away of a whole host of things that mattered to them. When light broke through the gloom, it emanated from somewhere in the past rather than somewhere in the present. The past wasn't perfect, all seemed to agree, but at least there they had experienced hope. From the past's many vantage points, it was possible to imagine a multitude of better futures. The hopes of the past were often quite worldly and transcended optimism's abstract ideals. Problems could be gradually dispensed with, and better things could take their place. Hard work would be rewarded. One's contribution would be recognised. Dangers would be overcome, and lives would become more secure and satisfying. However, by the time I spoke to them, much of the hope research participants felt during their earlier adult life had already fallen away.

The sense of decline that pervades this book may be discomforting, but it emanates from a commitment to representing the world as it is. It reflects the genuine material decline we see all around us, in our towns and cities, throughout our transport systems and in the institutions that once contributed greatly to the orderliness of the modern world. It reflects the obdurate insecurity that is such a regrettable feature of our lives today.[37] In analytical terms, it is also the product of a deep and objective analysis of our past and present. The old Enlightenment ideal of incremental social improvement – of a society driven forever forward by scepticism, evidence, scientific method and good government – no longer convinces us to anything like the extent it once did.[38] It is difficult to appraise our rapidly changing world with honesty and conclude that history seems to be carrying us progressively forwards, away from the horrors of the past and towards some hazy civilisational ideal that lies somewhere in the future.

This pervasive sense of decline – this sense of creeping lassitude, dilapidation, corrosion and decay, this slow-moving but persistent and apparently irreversible weakening and failure of virtually everything that once seemed stable and reliable – reflects both the objective socioeconomic position *and* the overall outlook of the men and women who are at the centre of this book. After innumerable false dawns and promised new beginnings, they cannot identity on the field of politics any force that might halt or even momentarily slow decline. Furthermore, it is clear to many research participants that, as a society, we have been falling for years.

The sense of decline expressed by participants often transcended the personal. Our discussions were principally concerned with politics, and few held back when discussing the declining quality of our politicians and the disappearance of virtue from the public stage. Others spoke of a perceived decline in community sentiments and cohesion. Some went as far as to paraphrase Thatcher's claim that society no longer existed, and everyone appeared to be out for themselves. There were also many more charitable and politically astute accounts of decline. Some acknowledged the diverse opportunities they appraised during their youth. Most were aware that jobs were once more plentiful, more secure and better paid. In their younger days, many had found it relatively easy to find good quality housing. Some had even bought houses of their own and watched on with surprise and excitement as the value of their homes continued to rise. Some could remember that the state had supported them as they moved between jobs or into training and education. Many unselfishly bemoaned the disappearance of these good things and worried for younger generations, who they were sure would find it much harder.

All seemed to concur that good things existed in the past, but very often the future seems dark and hostile. The very things that made life tolerable seemed increasingly out of reach. However, despite the very real problems they face, their lives tend not to be enshrouded in unrelenting gloom.

Things are not as simple as that. There are cracks of light here and there, and most continue to enjoy close personal relationships and a few minor consumer pleasures. Many of our conversations about life and politics had interludes of mirth and good humour. Nonetheless, their entirely reasonable identification of decline in many parts of their lives colours the ways they see and understand the past, present and future.

LOOKING BACK

This book is also concerned with the various ways nostalgia works, and the role it plays in the lives of the people as they appraise a world that seems to them increasingly bereft of hope and potential.[39] It identifies key themes that seem to structure the common experience of nostalgia. It explores the reasons why we remain attached to fleeting moments in time and how those moments become retrospectively imbued with significance and feelings of comfort. Why is it that we are transported back to these positive moments, afforded the opportunity to momentarily relive in the imagination specific biographical highlights and at the same time condemned by the painful awareness that those times cannot return?

For the men and women who contributed to this book, looking back affords a modicum of solace, familiarity, reassurance and warmth. Even on those occasions that it distorts or misrepresents a favoured reality, nostalgia aids the individual as she seeks to understand herself, her changing circumstances and her life in relation to others. Nostalgia is, then, a powerful tool of self-narration.[40] It assists our attempts to get to grips with who we are, where we're going, where we've been and what has truly mattered on our journey. It can help to solidify meaningful human relationships, and broadened out to a community level, it can encourage cohesion, loyalty, togetherness and common cause.[41] In this sense at least, working-class men and women are no different from others positioned elsewhere in our increasingly vertiginous social hierarchy.

Nostalgia can of course be trivial and inane and very often seems to carry no clear political content whatsoever. A quick glance across our assiduously dumbed-down and crudely commercialised popular culture will provide plenty of evidence to indicate that the substance of nostalgia can be appropriated, simplified and marketised. But that is certainly not all there is. As we will see, amid the rich diversity of our personalised memories lies our capacity to interpret and reconfigure, and it is these often quite complex processes that lend such memories a degree of political resonance.

To put it simply for the moment, nostalgia appears to be an outcome of our psyche's attempts to redirect conscious attention back to times that seem for some reason replete with positivity or towards images that seem suddenly important and worthy of critical and evaluative thought or simply towards images that might inspire particular sentiments or retrospective interpretations. Just as the psyche often pushes our conscious thoughts back to times of difficulty, fracture or threat – times that we might constructively reconsider and seek to fix or offset in some way – our memories of good times again suggest an unconscious drive to prompt reconsideration, re-evaluation and reassessment with the vague goal of guiding future thought and action.

These psychological processes are not straightforward. To accurately work through the meaning and purpose of such memories is a demanding task. Memories of traumatic events can be so disturbing that they cannot be accurately recalled.[42] Here, the psyche is attempting to protect the individual from the pain associated with those events. However, painful events of this magnitude tend not to be simply forgotten. Our psyche attempts to cathartically overcome the negativity of such events by repeatedly encouraging the individual to address and hopefully transcend the source of trauma. But because the traumatised individual cannot remember what actually transpired, she instead tends to remember *that which did not happen*. Symbols and themes indirectly connected to harmful events draw the individual back in the hope that the toxicity of such events can be dispensed with and the harmful memory either forgotten or disarmed.[43]

A vaguely similar process appears to be at work when remembering times of positivity, happiness and comfort. While there are no equivalent psychological barriers to remembering positive events from our past, it seems to be the case that nostalgic memories can change over time. While they continue to be imbued with positive sentiments, the specific events that inspire our nostalgic memories can become lost, or they can shift and change, leaving only a positive emotional residue, a general feeling that once seemed to have a fixed anchor in empirical reality. As we will see, nostalgic memories of the past are often only vaguely connected to actual events. Shaped and recontextualised by an incongruous superego that bombards us with paradoxical injunctions and a constantly shifting variety of threats and inducements, our memories are often inconsistent and, in many respects, indivisible from the thoughts, feelings and emotions they inspire.[44]

As we will see, the nostalgic memories of my research contacts tend to be imbued with overtones of security and the good things that flow from it, perhaps most obviously relaxation, confidence and the capacity to plan and imagine in ways that are not immediately overshadowed by the gnawing agitation, anxiety and fear that so often spring from insecurity. Put in simple Freudian terms for the moment, the manifest content of nostalgic memories seems to be much less important than their hidden latent content. Often the manifest content of the nostalgic memory – a family Christmas, attending one's first football match, a holiday abroad with friends, etc. – seems imprecise and unstable. Details are often forgotten, and memories of real events becomes gradually unfixed from the actuality of what took place. However, the real power of nostalgic memories seems to lie in their latent content. We remember not simply what happened, but how what happened made us feel. We remember the emotions that accompanied real events pregnant with symbolic meaning, and we remember the emotions drawn forth in the act of recalling them.

Looking back to good times seems to become more compelling and emotionally significant for individuals unable to identify anything positive in the present or the future. This is especially true of those individuals who have waved good-bye to the optimism and openness of youth. This is partly why I chose to focus on men and women between the ages of 45 and 60. Those I spoke to were not hopeless romantics, lost in daydreams about the fleeting beauty of youth, and nor were they maudlin depressives, dolefully condemning the world as it is now for not being the world as it was then. They were thoughtful people, and I enjoyed my time with them immensely. I learnt a great deal from our conversations, and I hope I have constructed an explanatory framework that at least partially illuminates the role of nostalgia in contemporary working-class politics.

The next chapter contains some rather basic points about what nostalgia is and how the concept has changed across time. This chapter also notes how the concept of nostalgia has become a common feature of the west's slow-burning culture wars.[45] The relatively recent politicisation of nostalgia tells us much about the forms of dialectical standstill that have paralysed and fragmented the contemporary west. The gradual unravelling of the modern social order has created fissures from which burst new or reconfigured forms of cultural hostility. Our notionally democratic political systems seem entirely incapable of generating movement or overcoming division. Nor do they display any interest in ditching present orthodoxies in order to embrace the challenge of building a better future. Often, it seems that more effort is given to the construction of imaginative new ways of defaming one's political opponents than to the grand project of reconstructing our economies and societies in the interests of the people. That some sections of the left aimed their fire at ordinary people invested in elements of the past and struggling to find a foothold in the present is also telling. In Chapter 2, we encounter some of the data upon which this study rests. First, we look at general themes. Overwhelmingly, the men and women I spoke to believe the past offered better opportunities and a more satisfying social experience. They also tend to be dissatisfied and frustrated with the realities of working-class life today, and they imagine the future to be typified by decline. Chapter 3 uses original data to expand upon these themes while focusing in particular on the sense of rootlessness that seems to underpin research participants' discomfort in the present and anxieties about the future. Chapters 4–6 attempt to contextualise and explain these sentiments by focusing, in various ways, upon the pace of change and its destabilising effects. Chapter 7 offers a brief but unfortunately not particularly uplifting conclusion that addresses the realities of our situation and the likely road ahead.

All that remains to be said at this stage is 'welcome to the book'. It is, I admit, a discomforting read. I certainly did not set out with this intention, but I remain committed to depicting the world as it is, warts and all. I hope you find something in it that helps you to better understand the perilous times in which we live.

1

THE NEW POLITICS OF NOSTALGIA

Nostalgia is now quite an old concept.[1] The ways that we understand and use the concept fluctuated slightly as it made its way into popular discourse.[2] At its core is a general meaning that centres upon positive memories of times past and a sentimental attachment to the various objects and events we associate with it. While it would be wrong to suggest that nostalgia is a constant feature of everyday vernacular, most people understand its essence and acknowledge it as a feature of their psychic lives. They are also capable of engaging in meaningful discussions about its characteristics.

Initially, nostalgia was presented as an ailment that afflicted only the weak.[3] Those stricken by it were believed to be paralysed by sentimentalism, laid low by a disabling home-sickness. Nostalgia was a virulent contagion that, without sensible pre-emptive action, could spread with remarkable speed, stripping the afflicted of their reason and separating them from reality. These early understandings of nostalgia gradually fell from favour. As the 20th century progressed, nostalgia came to be understood as a universally experienced and relatively harmless phenomenon. We all, at one time or another, reminisce about times gone by, and we can all be affected by the sudden appearance in our lives of objects that stir memories of key moments from our past.

Over time, nostalgia also came to be used in popular discourse as a means of capturing the experience of looking back with fondness to one's youth or to life's happier moments. It is often used to reference an emotional attachment to particular artefacts, genres and artistic forms symbolically connected to the past in some way.[4] Of course, in some instances, such attachments reflect a sentimental hankering for our younger days or to other periods of happiness and satisfaction. We might remain attached to the musical forms that moved us as we rushed to secure some sense of adult independence. We might continue to enjoy the old movies we watched with our parents as a child. We might cherish particular foods or routines or places that stir positive personal memories. Most people see nothing particularly worrying in such reminiscences. Rather, it seems to speak to what is to be human as we wander aimlessly to the grave. Nostalgia's broad emotional repertoire, its central injunction to contemplate and reconsider, our deep reliance upon our own unreliable memories and the apparently unbreachable gap that lies at the centre of subjectivity – all of these things appear to be at work as we find ourselves transported back to the most resonant events from our own personal histories.[5]

Like Marcel, the main character in Proust's *In Search of Lost Time*, we can be transported back to times past by a familiar sound, sight, taste or smell.[6] Hearing again the song that was playing when we first met a loved one might prompt pangs of nostalgia: the melody and the lyrics deepen and intensify precisely because they have become attached to such a happy and momentous event. Hearing such a song, however, tends not to inspire unalloyed joy. It is more likely that hearing the song prompts the complex amalgam of emotions that make nostalgia so compelling and so illustrative of our predicament as time bound and territorially situated subjects in an era of rapid, destabilising change.

Rather than prompt happiness, the song reminds us that we were happy *then*; we feel the comforting afterglow of positive but spent emotions. We might also feel an element of loss. The happiness we associated with the cherished moment lies in the past. It can only be revisited in memory. We return to the moment as a voyeur observing and vicariously enjoying our own reflected happiness. While the mental images of what transpired fray, warp and become discoloured with the passage of time, the event's emotional residue often proves resilient. We can return to that fateful moment in memory often, but we will never again experience the raw power of the authentic emotions that made this moment so memorable for us.

The word 'bittersweet' is often associated with nostalgic memories.[7] Certainly, such memories appear to contain elements of both happiness and sadness. This fusion of potent and seemingly contradictory emotions appears to be one of the reasons why we are drawn back to moments pregnant with both positive symbolism and vague suggestions of import. Our nostalgic memories are not aimless and nor are they entirely random. When we return in memory to such events, we are unconsciously searching of something. Our psyche encourages us to explore these events in the hope that we can happen upon something that might be of use to us. But what are we searching for? In a general sense, we are looking for something in our pasts that is absent in our present. We unconsciously hope to discover something that can be used to address our prevailing sense of incompleteness, a missing piece that might, we imagine, make us whole. But, of course, searching for something without clear shape and content can be an immensely difficult and occasionally frustrating task. It requires deep thinking, often in full knowledge that any discovery we make in the here and now might slip through our fingers in the near future. What is there, in the past, that I might need to reassure me and give me a sense of clarity and purpose? What truths might I discover that can assuage my perennial sense of incompleteness?

Generally, the nostalgic memories of those who took part in this study fell into two broad categories. First, nostalgic memories can be very specific. People occasionally offer very detailed descriptions of key events that inspire nostalgic memories, and they are usually capable of talking cogently about why the event has become important to them. People also discussed less precise but equally affective nostalgic memories. Here, rather than describe in detail what happened, people talked about positive periods in their lives. They offered a generalised account of, for example, the frivolity and fun of their youth, without focussing on specific events. They might, for example, mention holidays abroad or the joys of promiscuity and intoxication without recounting precise, illustrative memories.

However, these positive memories of particular periods in their lives could be equally evocative and inspire a good deal of rumination and thoughtful analysis. Predictably enough, those that talked with great affection about their youth tended to reference innocence, irresponsibility, the joys of being among friends and time dedicated to fun. But recalling this period of their lives often prompted some to acknowledge the practical support they received and the relative advantages available to them.

Of course, people are perfectly capable of moving quickly between specific to general nostalgic memories when talking about the relative freedom and positivity of youth. The same is true with regard to childhood, one's immediate family and the environments most commonly associated with one's early years.

Mothers and fathers were often remembered fondly. Conversations flowed from general observations about, for example, the characteristics of the parent and his or her selflessness, generosity and wisdom, to specific discussions about songs, mannerisms, clothes and so on or specific events that seemed, for the interviewee, to in some way capture the parent's essence.

Occasionally, the detail contained in these memories was remarkably precise. Some interviewees could remember, for example, what their mother had been cooking when they returned home with momentous news. They could remember what their father was wearing, and even his facial expression, in the midst of a symbolically important exchange. However, in this short text, I focus in more detail on generalised nostalgic memories. In terms of building a critical analysis of nostalgia, the researched community and the environments these people call home, general talk about happier times, times that seemed open, positive, hopeful, secure and comprehensible, fed into and often overlapped talk about politics and change.

But how should we understand nostalgia, and what role does it play in our psychic lives? Our super-ego often seems preoccupied with doubt, throwing at consciousness apparently infinite variations of how we might be viewed by others, how we might interpret past events, how we should have acted in those past events and the ceaseless variety of events we might face in the future. But the super-ego's apparent preoccupation with doubt is not a frustrating endpoint, designed to baffle us into submission or keep us awake at night churning over apparently meaningless events from the past or weird scenarios that might unfold in the future. Beneath the super-ego's ostensible desire to foment doubt lies a more fundamental psychological drive to identify and overcome threats of various kinds and move towards the clarity of resolution. In returning time and again to awkward moments from our personal pasts, we might develop more advanced forms of self-awareness and self-understanding and use these insights to move beyond whatever it is that is bothering us about those past events. In returning time and again to positive moments from our past, we are unconsciously driven to interrogate these moments in the hope of identifying something pregnant within them, something suggested but something that remains unspoken. We rethink who we are and why we are the way we are. We might also think about those things in our lives that have truly mattered. We might also consider where we are now in relation to where we were then. This specific effect seems closely connected to the relative pains of nostalgia. It is common to feel that we have, in life, lost our way somehow. It certainly seemed common for research participants to feel that the multifaceted positivity that surrounded their past selves had been withdrawn or had slowly dissipated. Encouraged to investigate such matters, many acknowledged the gaping hole of what could have been, of early promise unfulfilled, contentment lost, happiness squandered, the prospect of a perfect life somehow dashed on the rocks of circumstance.

The positive aspect of nostalgia is closely linked to the emotions evoked by reminiscence. We are often nostalgic for specific moments in which we were happy or moments that seem to symbolise a deeper or more enduring form of contentment. We find pleasure in revisiting these moments, even if in memory we assume the role of an observer rather than a participant. If the individual is momentarily unencumbered by the fidgety allure of screens, perpetual anxieties about work and the usual gamut of external demands, positive memories of the past can surface and the introspective reflection they inspire can begin.

There are also signs to suggest that we are predisposed to immerse ourselves in positive memories when seeking solace.

Interviewees frequently indicated that they tend to revisit nostalgic memories during moments of solitude, when the usually incessant demands upon their attention have briefly abated. Some also noted that nostalgia commonly intrudes on anniversaries and other noteworthy dates, when the habitual rhythms of their lives quietened, enabling them to drift off into deeper forms of contemplation. Part of this inclination was evidently practical. It is difficult to immerse oneself in deep memories if one is surrounded by others who might call upon your attention. Yet there were also indications that feelings of loneliness, vulnerability or detachment could encourage this particular kind of introspective rumination.

Nostalgia, of course, does not fall solely in the domain of individual experience. It also serves as a powerful bonding agent for groups of people. Numerous scholars have investigated the role of cultural nostalgia in the reproduction of national identities.[8] Elements of nostalgia underpin many cherished stories of national triumph, dogged determination and shared tragedies overcome. These stories can retain their power across generations. One does not need to have lived through the Blitz to be moved by, and subtly drawn towards, related stories of tragedy, stoicism, sacrifice, bravery and the power of collective endeavour. Such stories foster a sense of shared heritage, encouraging us to acknowledge our interconnectedness and our attachment to a particular place. These stories work in a broadly similar way to nostalgic memories, inasmuch as they do not need to accurately capture real events to be affective. Stories of our nation's past are often shot through with accounts of heroism, unity and moral superiority. They are also subject to deliberate manipulation.[9] However, our awareness of this manipulation does not necessarily mean that we will disavow the fundamental messages these stories carry. We may still be drawn to the themes of unity and heroism they emphasise, even if we are aware that they do not fully capture the true complexity of historical events. Brutal rationalism is certainly not guaranteed to dislodge belief. We do not immediately stop believing when faced with overwhelming contradictory evidence. We do not easily discard our objects of belief.

Nostalgia can be connected to emotional memory, auto-biographical memory, flashbulb memory and episodic memory.[10] Emotional and autobiographical memories are quite straightforward. Memories of emotions or memories that inspire emotions fall into the category of emotional memories, and memories that seem to define or in some way narrativise our lives tend to be categorised as autobiographical memories. Tulving, perhaps the most noted expert on autobiographical memory, suggests we need what he calls 'autonoetic consciousness' to enable us to revisit moments from our personal history. Autonoetic consciousness also allows us to use these memories to reflect upon our experiences, build self-awareness and prepare ourselves for future events.[11] While Tulving and other psychologists of memory tend to disregard Freud's conceptual repertoire, one can see how this work tends to confirm the claims made above.

Flashbulb memories are often tied to significant events and inspire powerful emotions. When we encounter something truly shocking, the event and the emotions it inspires can imprint themselves on our memory with remarkable precision.[12] Episodic memories also tend to be characterised by noteworthy events, but they are distinguished by their connection to particular times or places. Thinking of a beach we visited as a child might, for example, inspire a range of evocative episodic memories. Of course, as prominent memory scholars acknowledge, memories frequently defy neat categorisation and transcend rigid boundaries.[13] Rather, such categories have a principally academic function and help researchers and theorists bore down deeper into the intricacies of memory and the subjective experience of remembering.[14]

POLITICISING NOSTALGIA

Of course, these intricacies tend to be ignored by contemporary critics keen to use the concept of nostalgia to pore scorn upon their political opponents. Many critics have, in recent years, returned to the traditional conception of nostalgia and used it to condemn those they believe to be sentimentally attached to the past. It is now common to suggest that the individual *retreats* into nostalgia, which of course implies a defeat of some sort, or a speedy withdrawal in the face of what appears to be overwhelming oppositional forces. Of course, it is a mistake to confuse a tactical retreat with the cowardly act of fleeing. As we shall see, a sensible retreat can be used to better position oneself for future victories.

Most of the critics who have used nostalgia in this way are liberals of one sort or another, and for the most part, they have aimed their fire at those who appear to be on the 'conservative' side of the argument. These critics often position themselves as committed leftists, and the nature of their criticism suggests a general belief that criticising 'the right' for its nostalgia is a cogent strategy for worldly leftists untroubled by attachments to a past best left behind. However, very often, they end up criticising ordinary people for failing to sufficiently absorb and champion the liberal left's rapidly evolving worldview and future vision. They project regressive sensibilities onto ordinary men and women whose attachment to the past is far more nuanced than they care to imagine.

There is nothing inherently conservative about nostalgia. It is not too difficult to imagine how the left might use images and ideas from the past to construct a fundamentally better future. It was once commonplace to believe that the past has important lessons that can prepare us for the travails that lie ahead. It is only in our own disordered conjuncture that this traditional form of political education has fallen by the wayside. And there is no logical reason why ordinary men and women who could be won over to the cause of socialism should be chastised for looking to the past with fondness. One could be forgiven for assuming that it makes no strategic sense for the left to readily condemn ordinary people for the crime of being emotionally invested in their own histories and the places they call home. However, this apparently illogical strategy is fully in keeping with the general trajectory of the faux-radical post-1960s cultural left.[15]

The deployment of nostalgia as a tool of political critique is at once indicative of the growing cultural hostility that characterises popular politics today, while at the same time displaying a marked disinterest in overcoming the orthodoxies that bear down so heavily upon the majority. Using nostalgia in this way references our historical stuckness, our inability to move forward with purpose and the febrile atmosphere that ensues as diverse political constituencies – locked into unproductive patterns of thought and action – lash out wildly as frustration builds.[16]

As the 20th century progressed, liberalism displaced all other philosophical influences as it moved to the very centre of leftist thought. Today, it is usually assumed that committed leftists will be liberal on cultural issues.[17] It is worth keeping in mind that a similar process of philosophical colonisation has also beset the conservative right. Today, it is often assumed that all committed conservatives will be liberal on economic issues.[18] Despite the vocal hostility between the two groups, there is much they agree on. Indeed, these agreements between left and right enabled neoliberalism to shed its ideological skin, straddle itself across the political spectrum and emerge as basic economic 'common sense'. One might reasonably argue that the hostility between the liberal left and the conservative right reflects neoliberalism's ability to strategically displace economic dissatisfaction onto the field of culture in order to sustain the myth that genuine democratic political contestation continues.

The willingness of vocal leftists to disregard the fundaments of economic antagonism as they construct ethical critiques of their opponent's imagined motivations is highly suggestive of the problem of progressive politics at the imagined end of history.[19] Should ordinary people be chastised for their failure to support key features of contemporary cultural liberalism, even when their lifestyles are collapsing, when their neighbourhoods seem disordered and dangerous, when their futures look bleak and when they believe themselves to be increasingly locked out of mainstream social and political life?[20] Are poorly-resourced ordinary people supposed to magnanimously accept that their downward mobility is justified, and their problems are less important than those prioritised by the increasingly middle-class cultural left?[21]

The Brexit referendum offers a useful case in point. In its wake, many liberal critics suggested Brexit voters were regressive nostalgics obsessed with a distorted image of Imperial Britain.[22] Those who had voted to leave the European Union were apparently motivated to do so by a burning desire to propel the country back to the injustices of the past. Discomforted by multiculturalism and unsettled by the broad political acceptance of unrestricted cosmopolitanism, these voters had apparently sought to throw the movement of history into reverse and turn the clock back to a time in which people like them fared better. For these critics, nostalgia should be considered neither harmless nor universal. To be nostalgic was to be *pathologically* invested in the past and antagonistic to the supposed positive features of the present. It suggested a fear of freedom, difference and progressive change and a longing to return to the past's institutionalised prejudices.[23]

It is usually the stern voice of elite progressive liberalism that leads the chastisement of those who appear attached to the past. It pronounces with an admirable surety that the present is superior to the past. The past was strewn with horrors, and to look back with fondness is consequently to look back fondly upon bestial injustice. Of course, liberal progressives are partially correct. The past is indeed strewn with horrors. However, the past is a rather expansive terrain. Horror is only one of many things that can be found there. Making an ethical distinction between past and present tells us little of value, save for the fact that those making such a distinction are strangely assured that their own context-specific ethical judgements are beyond dispute, that it is reasonable to reduce both the past and the present to basic categories of ethical judgement, and that all who disagree willingly align themselves with horror.

We should also note that the surety of this pronouncement is indicative of the chasm that has opened between the elite progressive liberals who play a defining role in our media and dominate many of our institutions and the everyday people trying to navigate a path through the formidable turbulence of the 'real world'.[24] Certainly, those who contributed to this study were not at all convinced that our society was moving away from the injustices of the past. For them, economic injustice and declining standards of living were two of the most striking characteristics of the present. It was blindingly obvious to everyone that things had become a good deal harder for the vast majority, and this trend was expected to continue.

Of course, those who have sought to politicise nostalgia would immediately respond by claiming that those who have contributed to this study – principally white members of the working class – fail to recognise incremental cultural improvement because they have not been direct beneficiaries of this process. In fact, they have lost power as the privileges afforded to white people have been gradually reduced by a growing acceptance of multiculturalism. Rather than benefitting from historical privileges, they have been forced to complete with immigrants and non-white populations. And they have been found lacking. Their social status has declined, they are poorer, and their inadequacies have been revealed. Their refusal to acknowledge progress reflects their refusal to come to terms with a transformed world, less scared by cultural injustice and the absurd hierarchies of western modernity.

This argument, which I have reduced here to its basic elements, is indicative of the left's liberalisation and its growing distance from the realities of working-class life. The left liberals who make this argument are clearly happy to chastise members of the downwardly mobile working class for their failure to welcome the removal of their supposed privileges. Such claims are clearly underpinned by a general acceptance of perennial competition. Often it seems that the great hope is simply to remove pre-existing privileges and barriers so that when the gun is fired and the competition gets underway, the glittering prizes on offer on the consumer economy will be won by the most 'talented' and those truly dedicated to the pursuit of 'success'.

Liberal critics are, however, right to claim that nostalgia has become an important theme in contemporary cultural politics.[25] As we will see, nostalgia plays a significant role in shaping the attitudes of working-class men and women as they appraise the field of politics and as they begin to think about what needs to be done to improve the quality of their lives. However, it is not only the downwardly mobile working class that feels itself increasingly drawn to the past. Even in mainstream politics, there is an increasingly noticeable tendency to look to the past in the hope of identifying policies or practices that might allow us to overcome the obvious problems of the present. As I will argue in the latter half of the book, we increasingly look to the past because it seems to us orderly, logical and therefore comprehensible and often replete with a multitude of positive characteristics, both real and imagined. The past is perceived to be knowable. It bequeathed to us the forms of knowledge we use to understand our lives and experiences. The present, on the other hand, seems increasingly chaotic and irrational, its trends and processes indecipherable and often alienating. As soon as we believe ourselves to have gained some kind of grip on the present, our fleeting insight quickly evaporates as the present passes into history.

The future increasingly appears to us as an imponderable abyss of which we can know nothing. No clear signs of progress and improvement can be discerned. We appear to have lost the capacity to project images of bountiful new freedoms onto the darkness of this abyss. We no longer assume that future technologies will heal the natural environment and solve the world's ills. The field of politics no longer equips the people with coherent images of a positive future we can work towards and nor does it offer us feasible alternatives to what already exists. Adopting the standard cynical 'end of history' position that things are now as good as they ever can be, save for a little tinkering here and there, runs contrary to the by-now ubiquitous assumption that the lives of the majority are qualitatively worse than they were in the recent past. Without positive images, the future inevitably becomes more forbidding. The imagined unrestricted expansion of the negativities of the present merges with refracted representations of our own gnawing fears to create images of the future so terrible we feel compelled to turn away. Erasing the future fractures the sense of continuity upon which so much depends. Promulgating the belief that the future cannot surpass the present is ultimately toxic, and it is not at all clear that liberal democratic societies can sustain themselves in the absence of positive visions of the future.

A quick scan of working-class political history suggests that the politics of nostalgia tend to emerge as an identifiable trend in times of great turbulence, when material lifestyles are threatened and when the future seems likely to be absent of things judged to be of great value.[26] In this respect, and given the position we find ourselves in today, it is perhaps unsurprising that growing numbers of working-class men and women, especially those no longer in the first flower of youth, seem increasingly orientated towards the retrospective comforts of their personal pasts.

Anger, frustration, confusion and desperation abound. This is not to suggest that the silent majority is now beginning to stir and that the working class will soon reassume its role as the principal agent of history. Rather, it is important to note the simple but pivotal fact that nostalgia is playing a more significant role in the political life of the working class because we are once again passing through a time of great turbulence. The field of democratic politics is barren and uninspiring, and there is little for us to be optimistic about. Of course, one of the reasons why the contemporary field of politics is barren and uninspiring is because it is now populated by the most incompetent and ignoble political class in living memory. Nostalgia for a past in which the political class appeared to possess greater intellectual gravitas, loyalty and good sense – alongside the grand virtues traditionally associated with public service – is a common feature of popular discussion about how far we have fallen.

The forms of cultural critique I mentioned above are shooting vaguely in the right direction, but they fall well short of the target. As we will see, nostalgia does indeed feed into political attitudes, and it certainly affects the various ways in which the working class engage with national and local politics, trade unionism and other forms of political activism. However, those points conceded, there is little else of genuine value in these critiques. Overwhelmingly, they fail to understand the object of their critique and entirely misinterpret the function and focus of nostalgia in the political imagination of the contemporary working class. And crucially, the forms of cultural and political condemnation that tend to structure such critique tell us precisely nothing about how we might overcome antagonism and move towards an inclusive and harmonious future replete with the positive social features and supportive institutions that many believe are currently receding into history.

The ongoing criticism of working-class men and women for their perceived attachment to the past and their discomfort in the present has an obvious elitist character, especially given that those who have criticised working-class men and women for their nostalgia have clearly made no attempt to engage with working-class voters, or to understand the problems they face in building reasonably satisfying and secure lives.[27] Working-class Brexit voters were often portrayed as a dull-witted bovine herd manipulated by the right-wing press, too stupid to appreciate the obvious benefits of remaining in the EU's free-trade bloc, and blind to the positive forms of cultural change that stemmed from the EU's commitment to the looser movement of capital, goods and labour across the borders of its member states.[28]

Clearly hurt by the result and the perceived betrayal of a significant portion of the electorate, some liberal commentators went a good deal further. Those who had voted for Brexit were also depicted as ethnocentric nationalists threatened by multiculturalism and anxious that their social position might soon be usurped by hard-working immigrants keen to ascend the socio-economic ranks of a reconfigured Britain.[29] Fascism was resurgent and had clearly already seduced a good proportion of the electorate. Clearly, Brexit was a racist project.[30] All who had lent electoral support to it were tarnished by association.

A similar range of arguments arose in the wake of Donald Trump's election to the Presidency of the United States.[31] Across the world, a new wave of populism was beginning to swell.[32] Many populist movements mobilised elements of collective nostalgia or displayed their anti-technocratic orientation by acknowledging the commonly disavowed fact that things were getting worse across multiple measures. Hostility towards difference and a desire to turn back the clock were believed to be driving a resurgent white nationalism that threatened the very fabric of western liberalism.[33] However, in their rush to lambast post-crash populism, these critics often found themselves endorsing a liberal technocratic order that in its bone-chilling blandness and deep commitment to sociopathic austerity-based economic management had actually fomented the rise of the very populist movements they loathed.[34] As such, the widespread criticism of the new populism tended to reassert technocratic neoliberalism's claim to intellectual and moral superiority by presenting all alternatives to it as anti-democratic and potentially authoritarian.[35] The only viable path to a better future was to forcefully reject the vulgar populists and maintain one's faith that at some point in the future one of the mainstream neoliberal parties would actually introduce a programme that will finally benefit civil society.

However, while many liberal centrists continued to denounce all who proposed to step away from neoliberalism as bigots and closet authoritarians, it seemed that not all among their audience were convinced.[36] Many voters who lent electoral support to the new populist parties appear to have been motivated principally by the desire to arrest decline.[37] In the absence of serious proposals from the mainstream parties, growing numbers of everyday people were open to new voices from beyond the centre ground that proposed to ditch convention and refocus politics on relieving popular frustrations. The people clearly wanted change.[38] The mainstream parties promised only continuity.

Unsurprisingly, the changes proposed by the new populist movements varied enormously. However, as the years rolled by, it became clear that many of Europe's new populist movements were willing to accept the status quo. Their initial anti-elitist rhetoric and apparently incorruptible desire to free the people from harmful conventions seemed to fall away when they achieved office. Most were perfectly happy to accept the EU's institutionalised neoliberalism.[39] Most were also happy to accept the west's established foreign policy agenda. They had drawn support from frustrated voters who wanted change, but once in office, even their headline cultural policies were diluted or dispensed with entirely. Again, change candidates proved to be continuity candidates. Their promises of fundamental change had got them into power, but once in office, they restricted themselves to merely presentational changes that left neoliberalism firmly in place. Nothing, it seems, could be done to remove western nations from the orthodoxies driving their decline.

In times when political consensus coincides with decline, when the people feel insecure and ill-used and able to discern a multiplicity of tell-tale portents that herald further problems, they are far more likely to open themselves up to new ideas. They begin to listen to those who propose fundamental change. They pay attention to those who offer clear explanations of why things appear to be heading downwards and what might be done about it. They can be persuaded by those who focus on cultural conflict and who identify immigrants as the enemy. They can be persuaded that business elites and their sycophantic followers in government are the enemy. They can be persuaded to move to the right or to the left, and their judgements tend to be situated and subjective rather than constructed in relation to dominant post-Enlightenment accounts of logic and rationality. Claims are reality tested.[40] Does this explanatory framework tally with my own experiences? Is it robust enough to warrant my partial, contingent support?

In such a climate, rather than condemn those persuaded by nativist or ethnocentric accounts of decline, we might usefully turn our attention to the general absence of cogent and convincing accounts of decline that emanate from the political left, accounts that stress universality, togetherness, common cause and shared destiny, and offer people a positive image of renewal in which they can see material benefits for themselves and those they love. The left could have made a huge amount of political ground by promising deep and sustained public investment in the economy. A left that proposed to nationalise key utilities, bolster decaying infrastructure, create real jobs, boost the nation's productive capacity, improve urban environments, fix the housing crisis and determinedly set about the task of driving up standards of living would have earned the support of most working-class voters. Of course, the left's elites simply could not countenance any move away from the logic of neoliberalism. They refused to acknowledge decline or address the issues that really mattered to ordinary people. It was against this background that many working-class voters disengaged from the mainstream left and began to listen to other accounts of decline and renewal.

Working-class voters tend not to be nostalgic for authoritarianism or imperialism. Few ordinary men and women know much about Britain's imperial past, and a desire to reassert the privileges of 'whiteness' is really quite rare. Rather, when their nostalgia takes on a political aspect, it tends to look towards interventionist social and economic policy, full employment, high-quality healthcare and education, decent housing, lower levels of crime, functional public transport systems, and, crucially, the prevailing sense of security that emerged alongside these things. In short, they are nostalgic for the forms of safety, stability, orderliness and hope they associate with the modern world. These good things often appear to be disappearing from the world they presently inhabit.

An acknowledgement of fracture was often implicit in liberal criticism of the working class in the wake of the Brexit referendum. The progressive liberal left had finally lost the working class.[41] The working class – and especially those members of the working class who happened to have been born with white skin – seemed to no longer accept the tutelage of their long-standing self-appointed leaders.[42] The final break between working-class voters and left-leaning liberal progressives was, in many respects, to be expected. The relationship had been weakening for decades. The liberal left continued to tighten its focus on variants of cultural injustice, while large sections of the working class waited and hoped that someday soon the left would return to its roots and address the crippling economic injustice that cuts across all cultural groups.

It quickly became apparent that no attempt would be made to heal this fracture. Highly educated middle-class progressive liberals – the principal socio-political grouping of what is now routinely called the Professional Managerial Class (PMC) – had no interest in listening to the concerns of working-class voters.[43]

Nor could they bring themselves to display the magnanimity necessary to strategically acknowledge their own shortcomings in an attempt to heal division. Clearly, no accommodation could be reached with those who had so spectacularly failed to position themselves 'on the right side of history'. Instead, many PMC members of the liberal commentariat launched into a full-blooded condemnation of the ordinary people they once believed themselves to support. Those who did not vote for the liberal left's preferred candidates or accept their increasingly incoherent range of cultural commitments were irredeemable enemies poisoned by a concatenation of abominable bigotries.

In an increasingly Manichean political climate, 'winning' increasingly seemed to involve demeaning one's opponents, questioning their motives and misrepresenting their arguments before demanding their removal from the public stage. Logic, rationality, evidence and of course basic politeness and positive rhetoric seemed to be overtaken by instrumentalism and manipulative emotivism in what was the increasingly fraught climate of popular political debate.[44] Looking back from our current historical vantage point, it is difficult to avoid the conclusion that Brexit dragged to the surface a range of cultural antagonisms that had been bubbling away in the background for years. It also seemed to catalyse some relatively new antagonisms and propelled the country into a markedly hostile era in which no quarter was to be given.

In the high tempo cut and thrust of battle, nostalgia was shorn of its universal character and again became an indicator of underlying pathologies. No longer was it suggestive of the individual's sentimental but reasonably harmless and apolitical attachment to times past. A reconfigured conception of nostalgia has now become a key weapon of political critique, and it is usually deployed by those on the liberal left and aimed at their antagonists on the 'far right'.

The modern political spectrum has of course, since the advent of neoliberalism, undergone a great deal of change. The 'far right' now often seems to be a strangely featureless category into which all who do not immediately agree with the liberal left's evolving cultural agenda might be ruthlessly shunted. One might reasonably judge the liberal left's willingness to daub its various antagonists with the symbols of absolute evil to be a poorly conceived strategy. Labelling our various opponents Nazis dilutes and disguises the far right's most morally objectionable goals and viewpoints and tends to erode our collective ability to recognise and respond to those elements of the 'far right' that truly deserve that designation.

The evolving shape of the political right is perhaps most clearly seen in the rise of what is now routinely called the 'alt-right'. Clearly, this new grouping has sought to cut itself free from the decaying remnants of 20th century fascism and modern ethnocentric nationalism. It is media savvy, comparatively youthful and often seeks to lampoon its opponents. Clearly, the alt-right have learnt many lessons by carefully observing the strategies of the post-sixties left. Many of its most vocal advocates routinely position themselves as a counter-hegemonic force dedicated to resisting and displacing a stuffy and sanctimonious liberal left from its comfortably ensconced position at the head of many of our core institutions.[45] For the alt-right, the liberal left has become 'the establishment', whereas they imagine themselves to be daring cultural insurgents dedicated to the returning power to the people.

The left has also changed a great deal. Competition and division seem to have replaced solidarity and common cause as foundation stones for the left's ideology and practical politics. Particularism and individualism have replaced universalism and collectivism, and few appear to retain any principled ambition to either replace or significantly reform the contemporary capitalist economy. It is also important to note that many on the left believe that a loose confederation of social movements has replaced the multi-ethnic working class as the principal agent of progressive social change.[46]

Where once the left was synonymous with the multi-ethnic working class and saw itself as a movement dedicated to advancing its economic and cultural interests, now the left seems determinedly middle class, both in its character and in its policy aspirations. Large sections of the left now seem to have given up entirely on the working class. Indeed, some leftists seem relieved to have been liberated from the traditional pretence of cross-class alliance and accord and free to engage in the forms of haughty cultural condemnation commonly associated with the conservative right. And, of course, as many readers of this book will know, hardly any mainstream leftists continue to advocate for redistributive socioeconomic policies. Instead, most are steadfast defenders of a decaying neoliberal order that actively harms the interests of the majority.

These changes are tied to the general enculturation of politics, a process that separates the realm of political economy entirely from democratic debate and oversight. As we moved into the final decades of the 20th century, all mainstream political parties accepted the evolving framework of neoliberalism. All agreed that the state should abandon direct investment and instead encourage the private sector to invest. All accepted that corporate and investment elites possessed the boundless creativity to drive growth and technological innovation. All mainstream political parties accepted these new 'truths'. If they did not, they were quickly jettisoned from the new conformist and increasingly technocratic mainstream.

As virtually every mainstream politician accepted the magical properties ascribed to markets, the field of democratic politics buckled and shrank. While post-war governments had before them an array of potential policy routes, governments in the 21st century faced a trimmed down and rather dismal policy vista. Today, it often seems like nothing much can be changed. We are constantly told that we have run out of money.[47] The state no longer has the wherewithal to intervene. And, if the private sector cannot be encouraged to invest, we must accept decline. Often, the basic message seems to be that only profit and rent-seeking elites can save us. The reality of contemporary political and financial power is hidden from view. Mainstream politicians have been defanged and domesticated. Most seem happy to relinquish their traditional role as aspiring architects and engineers of a future Britain that might yet be brought into being.

Buoyed by the popular belief that endemic careerism cannot be overcome and the best that can be hoped for is that openly venal and corrupt politicians might be turned out of office at the next election, mainstream politicians seem to cheerfully accept their revised remit. No longer politicians in the true sense, they became mere custodians of what already exists. Apparently happy to be in the limelight for a brief while, and with one eye on the financial opportunities available in the private sector once they shuffled off the public stage, they set about the work of absorbing popular dissatisfaction while administering decline.

As we pressed on deeper into the 21st century, it became gradually clearer that virtually all mainstream politicians agree on economic matters. Policies external to the neoliberal orthodoxy were rarely discussed and then seemed to disappear entirely. However, a few differences remained on cultural matters, and as time wore on these rather shallow cultural issues gradually seemed to subsume the entire field of democratic politics. Of course, one might reasonably claim that democratic politics has become increasingly theatrical, but it seems to have become so in order to maintain the pretence that Britain continues to possess a vibrant and inclusive democratic system in which the people ultimately determine the direction the nation takes as it moves painfully into the future.

The austerity that followed the 2008 global financial crisis did not end. Instead, it became a durable and apparently inescapable norm. Economic policy aspirations these days seem to hinge upon the reduction of the deficit. As many readers will know, this is an economically illiterate and self-sabotaging aspiration that reflects the triumph of ideology over reason and evidence.[48] Where it has proven impossible for government ministers to reduce the deficit without driving the nation further into a prolonged social crisis that would sabotage their chances at the next election, they have tended to adopt the more practical strategy of attempting to prevent the deficit from growing to the extent that it begins to worry 'the markets', a vague agglomeration of global financial interests that have assumed de facto control of the nation's economic decision-making. Manipulating interest rates and taxes, cutting spending and selling off state-owned assets seemed to be the only levers in the economic engine room that, after nearly half a century of compulsory neoliberalism, government finance ministers still felt able to pull upon.

Cynicism was, by this stage, already embedded as a key feature of British popular culture. Most seemed to assume that the Westminster scene simply couldn't give birth to anything of any great value to the people. Nothing of any consequence could come to fruition. The people seemed to await a genuine leader capable of inspiring faith. However, few could summon up the belief that such a leader could ever truly arise from the grey morass of Westminster party politics. The vast stores of money accrued by vested interests and the huge power of systems of popular management and control could not disguise the fact that the search for truth and justice had been abandoned.

Apathy and cynicism did not immediately destabilise democratic politics. Technocratic neoliberalism had stripped faith from the electoral system. At election time, few were able to suspend disbelief and look forward with optimism to a new government committed to righting wrongs and driving the nation forward to a new era of prosperity. Events had rendered such hopes impossibly naive. But without faith, without a widely held belief that things could be changed for the better, the democratic system seemed to take on a rather ghostly aspect. It was all surface, all presentation, with absolutely no substance. It was all soundbites, photo opportunities, bland identikit interviews and insipid debates about topics that really didn't matter. In opposition, politicians were free to moralise on matters of the day and defame their opponents as unfit to govern. In government, they were quick to point out that nothing could be changed, and expectations needed to be 'realistic'.

Stripped of its substance, democratic politics stumbled on as if nothing had changed. People continued to vote. Certainly, voter turnout statistics did not suggest a broad withdrawal of interest in and commitment to the electoral system. But the true situation was a good deal more complicated. Without faith that the party-political system could deliver positive change, electoral politics became increasingly negative in its overall orientation. Rather than positively endorse a party and its policy programme, one now tends to vote for the party one is least appalled by. On election day, our great abiding hope is that the least-worst party will be able to form a government. It is a path that leads inevitably downwards.

Cultural politics retained a façade of forthright contestation, mostly because there still appeared to be some hope that various surface aspects of culture might be changed. Immigration remained a hot issue that animated a large portion of the electorate, but the debate on immigration was largely a debate about its perceived cultural effects. The brutal economic, ecological and geopolitical forces that propel populations around the global in search of a better life could be neither debated nor understood. The possibility of intervention in the daunting global economic and geopolitical processes that contextualise immigration is simply no longer on the agenda.

As the years passed and light failed to break through the gloom, most voters became inured to the new cultural politics. Many seemed to form the view that the Labour Party was socially liberal and the Conservative Party less so. But even these vague characteristics could not be relied upon. Both parties appeared willing to move to either the left or the right on culture if there appeared to be some electoral advantage in doing so. The Labour Party leadership was willing to take the knee in support of Black Lives Matter but promised to be tougher than the Conservatives on immigration. The Conservative Party were happy to talk tough on illegal immigration but seemed incapable of placating their base by stemming the flow of immigrants entering the country. All of this seemed to reinforce the view that the post-crash political class had become paralysed by fear and lacked the confidence to do anything more than issue vague promises while condemning their opponents.

None of the main political parties were understood in relation to their economic policies. This was of course because on economic matters the parties were virtually indistinguishable. But underneath these general perceptions lay a growing recognition that the two main parties of British politics were not actually two parties at all. The shouting was just for show. The Conservative Party couldn't reduce immigration and nor could it defend the nation's cultural traditions. The Labour Party couldn't advance the cause of social justice. All they could do was meekly talk about their aspirations and perhaps introduce one or two banal, presentational policies that changed virtually nothing. Despite the incessant grand-standing, key protagonists in both parties seemed quite closely aligned. The sole overriding concern was simply to keep the system as it stood broadly on track despite the fact that it appeared to be heading downhill at considerable speed.

It was against this background that nostalgia was refitted with a new range of symbols and associations and deployed as a weapon in the ensuing culture wars. The past no longer seemed to function as a vast arena of events, processes and contexts from which we might learn. Instead, it was presented as a space of irredeemable injustice, a simplified moral judgement that reflected the institutionally established post-WWII fear that past horrors might break free from the constraints of time and re-emerge in the present. Of course, as they joined their antagonists in the act of manipulating the past's imagery, these critics were really attempting to shape the politics of the present and the future. Beneath the pro-gressive rhetoric, this new strand of liberal critique forcefully demarcated the limits of progressive change. The people must become more inclusive, welcoming and charitable despite the fact that the apparently inescapable neoliberal framework is a brutal competition that militates against such things. The process of reconfiguring the state and the economy to ensure the continued primacy of oligarchic and financial interests could not be interrupted. No matter how bad things became, a genuine political intervention from either the left or the right would make things immeasurably worse.

The continued destruction of the social democratic wel-fare state could not be brought to an end. The perennial insecurity that accompanied fully marketized social life could not be assuaged. To dispense with progressive neoliberalism was to invite horror. Left populism would take us back to the gulag and right populism to the concentration camp.[49] Our only hope to cling on to what is valuable in the present and prevent the reemergence of the horrors of the past was to reassert our commitment to parliamentary capitalism and have faith that liberal elites would gradually reform its shallow, presentational cultural programme and magically create a socially just world amid growing desperation and material decline.[50] Of course, while an increasingly strident liberalism continued to diversify its strategies of cultural repression, it could not fully quieten those who wanted to break free from the orthodoxies of the neoliberal age. The degradation of western societies and growing fears about the future would inevitably foment the forms of ethnonationalist reaction that liberalism fears most.

It is easy for those on the left to fall into the trap of believing that the ruling ideology is a product of the political right. But the ideology of progressive neoliberalism fuses elements of liberal left thought with market fundamentalism, and it is this ideology that rules.[51] Thus, contemporary politics is alive – at least notionally – with constant chatter about the ethical management of cultural life but entirely silent on how our economies might be democratised or revolutionised. The culture wars rage while the investment class goes quietly about the business of inflating assets, collecting rent and compound interest, suppressing wages, outsourcing labour, avoiding taxes, disempowering or domesticating trade unions, corrupting democratic politics, privatising natural resources, building private armies and amassing vast stores of wealth. Our corporations incorporated a shallow version of EDI into their management discourse and now often seek alliance with cultural interest groups, but they remain utterly committed to maximising profit, privatising the commons and enriching investors.

Liberal critics were right to suggest that nostalgia was playing an increasingly important role in shaping the political outlook of ordinary people, but rather than seek to accurately identify why people were becoming nostalgic, what they were nostalgic for and what their nostalgia might tell us about politics, they fell into the predictable trap of self-righteously and pre-emptively condemning what they didn't understand. Brexit, Trump and the reemergence of populism across Europe provoked not a desire to fully comprehend why ordinary voters might lend their support to unconventional parties and projects but forms of ideological condemnation that sought to affirm progressive neoliberalism as the only viable response to the hostility, anger and pain that had been whipped up by neoliberal universalism. Rather than self-aware socialism locking horns with the ruling neoliberalism, a notionally 'progressive' version of neoliberalism locked horns with a resurgent but market-friendly right-wing nationalism to again propel history further along a path of diminishment and degradation.

The recent repoliticisation of nostalgia also omits another crucial insight. Encouraging the people to enjoy the turbulence of the present will not cure them of their attachment to a past that appeared more stable, comprehensible and gratifying. Certainly, the mockery heaped upon working-class voters for lending their support to various populist movements does not appear to be bearing fruit for an embattled liberal class clearly anxious about where a return to history might lead us. Nostalgia springs from lack. The forms its takes tell us something important about what is missing in the present. We will only be in a position to address nostalgia's perceived negative effects when we finally give people what they need to live contentedly in the present.

In Lacanian terms, the terror of the real subsides when we accept the fictions of a symbolic order.[52] The truths that seem to structure the symbolic order give us something to believe in. We suspend disbelief and utilise its diverse range of meanings as we attempt to make sense of our lives, identities and experiences. However, symbolic orders cannot sustain our commitment indefinitely. Their supposed truths breakdown as we withdraw our faith and begin to tarry again with the gnawing anxieties, insecurities and paralysing cynicism that are the product of the constitutive lack that lies at the centre of human subjectivity. We once again recognise that most of the symbolic order's supposed truths are mere stories and return to a position of grudging disbelief. And this is what we see as the modern age's symbolic orders break apart: a disorderly world of competing truth claims, a cacophony of disconnected stories that solicit our faith but none of which has the power to burst through ossified cynicism to capture our hearts and justify our devotion. Desperate to believe but obliged to imagine every object of belief irredeemably flawed or already corrupted, and the tools we might have once used to appraise truth claims redundant, we turn inwards as we await something magical that will finally dispel cynicism, demand our re-engagement and justify our renewed faith.

It is vital that we believe again. A new truth project must be constructed that can burst through the smog of postmodern cynicism that enshrouds western culture. We need to reimagine the future and convince the people of the justice of our vision and efficacy of our plans. The task is huge, but we must try. Our fidelity to this task will determine whether it is indeed possible to shift the trajectory of history from decline to incline. It is also vital that we construct new stories and images of what can be achieved in the present. And this is one of the many reasons why a new left needs to quickly emerge from the ashes of the old. In the next chapter, we will use the words of those who took part in this study to more accurately capture the true politics of nostalgia.

2

FEARING THE FUTURE

This chapter presents quotes that address the interplay between past, present and future. These quotes have been chosen because they contain elements common throughout the overall sample. As we shall see, interviewees were overwhelmingly willing to acknowledge that the past was not perfect, but they nonetheless believe it to have been better than the present. Similarly, interviewees tended to express the belief that, for people like them, the future is likely to be significantly worse still. Overwhelmingly, the data suggest that many working-class people believe that community sentiments have declined, the world of work has become less satisfying and rewarding, the political class is increasingly corrupt and self-interested, declining living standards have negatively affected most facets of their lives and that future generations will struggle as these trends inevitably continue.

Paul is 50 years old.[1] He is married with two teenage children. He works in sales. On the surface, Paul seems reasonably affluent. He owns his own home and drives a good-looking and reasonably new car. However, beneath the surface, lives such as Paul's are rarely picture perfect. He struggles to meet his mortgage commitments, a large monthly car payment and outstanding credit card debts. High inflation and rapidly rising interest rates have inhibited his lifestyle enormously, and he is now struggling to make ends meet. Increasingly disinterested in his job, he'd like to retire or somehow find his way into a job that gives him some sense of satisfaction. For now, however, that remains out of the question.

Paul's house is located around two miles from the estate on which he grew up. His mother still lives there, and he has a sister who moved south many years ago. Paul went to the local comprehensive school, and he is still well known in this part of town. There can be little doubt that, despite his outward signs of consumer success, Paul remains working class. He displays the mannerisms, values and behavioural norms of the regional working class. His career has taken him away from the estate, but he remains tied to the area and its people at a fundamental level. Paul has clear memories of poverty, and he faced a range of associated troubles during his youth. Paul and I talked a lot over the course of the project. He had a lot to say and helped me greatly by introducing me to others. I found Paul to be great company. However, as we walk around the old neighbourhood today, he becomes gradually more contemplative. He had this to say:

'We've pushed back the mortgage three times. When it started, I thought I'd be free of it when I got into my fifties. Now I'm going to be paying until I retire. Our mortgage rate has gone right up. We've cut right back on everything. We [Paul and his wife] were talking about selling, and maybe renting somewhere instead. The boys, though: there's no sign of them moving out anytime soon. I can't do it to them. We still need the bedrooms. We'll [Paul and his wife] just keep working as long as we can'.[2]

Paul works around 15 miles out of town for a multifaceted, nationwide company. He has worked there for almost 20 years.

'I've been panicking about it, all of it. It weighs on you, doesn't it? The car, I'm tied in for three more years. I need it for work. The price of cars is totally nuts. Our lass is taking extra hours. Even with the supermarket now, we are watching every little thing. We used to have money to spare. The stuff we've bought over the years. Not now'.

'There's no question, [life] is harder now. I know I'm lucky. I know other people are struggling more. But when I look back, I guess it seemed as though we had more opportunities. We had chances to do better... Everyone was in the same boat. No one really had much, but somehow it didn't seem to matter, did it? Life has been pretty good to me, overall. I had some troubles, but I was a happy kid. We'd be out playing football, take our bikes off to the park. Then, when we'd left school, we'd be out drinking and dancing and all the rest of it. All the things you get up to when you're young. Off to Ibiza for a week, Amsterdam. Everyone together, loads of us, that's what I remember'.

Today, Paul has a lot to say about his children. His sons have not proven to be particularly academically inclined, and the path ahead for them is unclear.

'My youngest leaves school this year. Me and the wife are pushing him to go to college, just so as he has a chance of getting a decent job. Something in the building game, something practical. We'll see how it goes. He isn't a bad lad, but he just isn't bothered. He doesn't know what he wants to do. But he has to do something. I worry for him, obviously. I don't want him going off the rails. I've seen it so many times. I know what can happen. We will help them out as much as we can. But you want them to do something for themselves. Get out there and do something. Grow into men'.

'I wanted them to get into computers, something in technology. That's where the jobs are going to be. But he is not minded to that kind of stuff. The old trades are the only thing he showed any interest in. People will always need plumbers, electricians, builders maybe. If he can get the qualifications. Better that than in sales, sitting around in an office. I don't want them in that world. But I don't know. Any job would do at the moment'.

'People give shit to young lads today, but honestly, these lads, how are they going to afford a house? How're they going to, I doubt know, get married, start a family? Where are they going to live? Look at this estate here. You can't even get a council house now. It's so hard. We are trying to get them into a job, but the jobs, how do you save for anything on a tenner an hour? And a lot of them jobs aren't even full-time. I don't want them working in them jobs. I don't want them getting ripped off. But I don't want them sitting about doing nothing neither'.

'That's what I'm nostalgic for: descent jobs. Put that down. We got jobs easy. I wasn't great at school, but there were all kinds of jobs. If you wanted to work, you could work. Everything I got, I worked for. You put the hours in, it pays off. Most of the lads I come up with did something, you know, got jobs, families, houses. Now, kids have got to go off to university just to stand a chance. It's fucked, all of it'.

'It's a generation thing, isn't it? They've got iPhones and Playstations but there's no decent jobs, no chance of getting a house. You've got to go to college, even if you want to be a plumber or a bricklayer. There's no apprenticeships now. [You have to] work your arse off to get a job that pays you just enough to eat, end up in a bedsit on some shithole estate, get broken into every time you leave the house... Would I make it off this estate if I was young today? Unlikely, isn't it?

It's a fucking hopeless place. It's sad what happened. This place used to be alive, I don't know, positive. Just better'.

'I think back to the laughs we had here. There was some bad lads about, no doubt. No shortage of bad stuff going on. We got up to all sorts of capers. But it was all just for a laugh. I think, when you're that age, you don't see the poverty... I knew people were poor; there was obviously people who had nowt. I don't know, it just, it didn't seem as serious, not to us as kids. That's how it is when I look back. I think if you push me to really think about it, I can remember that, you know, yes, there was poverty. Some of the kids at school were obviously just in really bad situations. But overall, I'd still say it was a better, happier time. Maybe I don't focus on the bad. You try to forget the bad. But when I look at this place, I just see things getting worse, not better'.

Many of those I spoke to didn't want to talk about politics. They avoided talking about it in their everyday lives because it made them angry. It led to arguments and broken friendships. Generally, most people believed that in the past there were politicians of a higher quality, and they could get quite animated when discussing perceived ongoing political failure.

'I can't mate, it just does my head in. I can't even watch the news these days. It's been bad news for twenty years, hasn't it? [Politicians] are just the worst kinds of people. I can't stand them. All parties. Liars and thieves. I voted Conservative last time. First time I ever voted for them. Never again. I'm not voting. There's just no point. They'll never do anything for the working man. Never'.

'If I remember back, I think I voted Labour because they had some people in there who seemed, well, just decent I suppose. Sensible, like they wanted to make things better, you know? They were going to stand up for ordinary people. Make sure there were jobs, make sure everything worked. The Conservatives, I never really understood. I just never even considered voting for them. They never cared, you could just see. Now, every politician I see on TV, you can see they're just lying to you: "we're going to do this or that". It's all bollocks. They're going to do fuck all. They're going to do fuck all, and things are going to get worse. Vote Labour, total shit. Vote Conservative, total shit. Honestly, you can't look at the fucking shower we've got now and say there's someone there who isn't out for themselves. They just seem like they're winging it, they've got no idea what they're doing, smiling at the camera, talking shite'.

When pushed to discuss contemporary politics, many others mirrored Paul's dark cynicism. Kate is 53. She works as a travel agent and is married with two adult children. She and her husband live in a three-bedroom semi in pretty good part of town.

'I think things have been heading downhill for ages. Wherever you look, it's getting worse. They've been laying off people at work, and I half-expected to be out. I'm tired of it. It's so exhausting. We used to have a right laugh, but we've lost people. Friends of mine left, and there's so much monitoring and targets and everything. But what are you going to do? What else is there? I'm too old to move now'.

'I hate talking about politics. No one has a nice word to say about them [politicians]. Everyone's so angry. You do your best to just ignore it. That's what we do up here, [we] make the best of things. I just wish something would come along. People are waiting for something to happen, that's what I think. Waiting and waiting. Waiting for something that never comes. "Things will get better, things will get better": You're hanging on to the hope'.

'I used to think, everything in the future will be great, everything hi-tech and beautiful. People were so optimistic. People believed, you know, that if you put the work in you can get on. I know I shouldn't complain. But there's people I know who have just given up. That's what it seems like. There are so many problems, you don't know where to start. The optimism has gone'.

Arthur is 51. He is a good friend of Paul, quoted above. Arthur has worked in the building industry since leaving school. For the last 12 years, he has had his own company, which is mostly engaged in small-scale domestic work. He works alongside his younger brother, Greg, who is also quoted in this book.

'It's all gone to shit. Everything. Name one thing that's got better in the last ten years. Everything is harder. There's more competition [at work]. Even for small jobs. We're working harder for less money. We're taking on pretty much any job we can now. And it's not just me. Maybe you'll say I shouldn't be complaining, but something needs to be done quick. This country is fucked. The prices of things, it's just gone nuts. I'm working six days most weeks. I'm one of those people who goes around turning the lights off, turning off the heating, trying to save as much as I can. And no-one's doing anything. No one cares. How did we get in this mess, eh? I used to think things would keep on getting better, but everything gets worse now. The town centre, all the big shops have shutdown. It's all takeaways and charity shops. Dandridge Street [the main neighbourhood thoroughfare] is a disaster. Have you seen it? Shitty little shops, lots of immigrants standing around, litter everywhere, crime up, people getting pissed, potholes, the guttering's all smashed in, the pavements are a mess. There's not many left around our way. Everyone moved out. I go back to see my Mam's sister now and then, but that street, I don't know anyone now. They don't look after the street, their houses. That used to be a proper neighbourhood, that'.

'The way things are going, I don't know. There needs to be a revolution or something. The politicians can't be arsed. They're not going to fix anything. More immigration, higher prices, shit jobs. We are turning into a third world country. There's so much wrong. You tell me when there was ever more going wrong. I think now, the age I am, I'll just hanging on 'til retirement. My knees are falling apart but I'll keep working. Have to. But my young one? And what if he has kids? Doesn't bear thinking about. Climate change now, and Christ knows what'll happen with the economy. Uncontrolled immigration. Who's going to fix it? Who is going to look after the citizens of this country? No-one is going to fix it, so it'll keep getting worse… Greg [Arthur's brother] was saying he's going to vote Labour. We had a whole argument about it. Labour isn't going to change anything. It's just all bollocks, the political system. We've been robbed, for years it's been'.

I pushed Arthur to expand on immigration:

'Look, I'm not racist, right? I'm not. I couldn't care about any of that. But so many have come over now, it just doesn't make any sense. There's so much competition in the building game nowadays, and anyone can see wages have gone down. I don't mind immigrants if they come in and work and get involved. We've had Africans around here for a couple of years, and most of them are nice, good people as far as I can tell. They say hello, they go to the church. I even saw some of them picking up litter. Brilliant. Not even locals do that. But we've had problems around here, big time. Problems at the school, grooming gangs, problems with rapists, drugs, massive drugs problems we've had, even prostitution, which you never used to see'.

'What I've got from politics recently is that no one plans to do anything about it. I thought Boris [Johnson] was going to do something, but things have got worse. Stop the boats [a key Conservative rallying cry in 2023]! You've got to be joking. They can't tell their arse from their elbow. They're getting rich off immigration so it's not going to stop, is it? More immigrants, lower wages, worse everything, no money to pay for stuff.

Round and round we go. And you're asking about the future? That's what I see. A low-wage economy, no skills. No NHS, no decent schools. Everything falling apart. And I guess no real sense of community or who we are. No sense of the history, just completely different from what it's been. And look at this place! Why isn't this stuff getting fixed? We can't even fix the roads. Potholes everywhere. I mean, that's not an expensive job, is it? It's not that they can't afford it; it's just they can't be arsed. They don't care. Couldn't care less about our roads up here'.

'People like me will be gone. That's what we are, the last of the Mohicans, the last of the working class[...] You used to be able to do well in the building game. The last chance for people to do well, without the education and the qualifications and all of that. So we are dying out. Like this town is dying'.

Dennis is a 53-year-old joiner and kitchen fitter. He has two adult children and recently became a grandfather.

'I'm not one of these who get all misty eyed for the good old days. I've got nowt to say about everything being great when I was young. What I'm nostalgic for is just a world that worked. It's bullshit that things were perfect. Nothing was perfect when I was growing up. But the key thing was that it worked. It did, didn't it? All of it! The schools worked, the buses worked, travel, jobs, all of it. I'm not saying "perfect". I'm saying "worked". I hated school, but it worked. When I left school, there were jobs. This was in the middle of Thatcher! Millions on the dole, strikes and all the rest of it. But we got jobs. All the lads I left school with got jobs. We all got on, and this is what I'm saying: it just worked. We were raised to work. We got jobs, got houses, married, kids and just got on with it, with life. Even the dole then, it worked. And now, nothing works! The schools don't work, the city doesn't work, the council doesn't work, the unions don't work: nothing works!'

I asked Dennis if he thought the world was becoming more disorderly:

'Yes, that's it! It's disorder. There was order and now there's none. No one knows what they're doing. No one knows what they're supposed to be doing. Everyone's blagging it, thinking of themselves. It's mental, because people are all over the place nowadays. I know people that just don't have a clue, don't know what's going on, don't know what to do. Just, I don't know, just lost'.

'I blame the rich. I blame politicians. All those wankers down there, they're all to blame. Grabbing what they can for themselves. I mean, I don't know anything about politics. If it's on the telly, I'll turn it off. They're just wankers. I can't explain it. Something happened, and now we're fucked'.

At 60 years old, Colin was the oldest man involved in the study. Colin enjoyed a long career working for the local council but is now on permanent sick leave. He suffers from diabetes and heart problems. Colin divorced 12 years ago and moved into a small terraced house not too far from the neighbourhood where he grew up.

'I voted Labour when I was younger. Never would've voted for Thatcher. She destroyed this whole area. It started with her, really. Things got worse after she came along. And Blair. I voted for him the first time, but he was just a sign of things to come. They're all just awful really, aren't they? Have been for ages. Where do you look to find some sense and a decent plan? We had some good old characters, years ago. Labour was for the people. This whole area, full employment. The council was great, loads of services, good quality, the town was clean and tidy, the schools were better then. Less crime. What I think we lost is that sense of decency. No one looks out for each other like they used to. Everyone's just strangers, and it really didn't used to be like that when I was growing up. We had some sense of being in it together, and I thought one day soon we'll get a good Labour government, and they'll look after us and push us forward. I was hopeful, and that's gone now, totally gone. I shouldn't have thought I'll vote again. Who would you vote for?'

'There's no question, our politicians are worse. It's just a job now. They don't care about ordinary people. They don't care about, just improving things, improving the country. When you see them on TV, they seem, I don't know, untrustworthy. Like they're trying to trick you or get one over on you. They won't answer questions. They want to convince you that they care: "Don't worry! We're going to help you! Don't worry, we'll fix things!" But how can you believe them? Look what's happened to this town. Everything is useless. Nothing works. Go out and look at the back lane: rubbish piled up, mess, litter, mattresses, old bits of furniture. It's a fire risk. The council can't do anything like what it used to. It's been stripped back to the bone. A friend of mine got burgled a couple of weeks ago. But the police don't care. Dangerous times'.

Colin had a lot to say about the decline of community sentiments:

'I think, if I look back, I grew up in the best time. My parents worked all the time and still had nothing. My Dad, he worked in the shipyards. My Mam worked so hard to give us a good start, she really did. She didn't really have anything for herself. And I think the schools were better. The teachers were tough and I'm not saying it was perfect. But look at me; I got through it and left school with qualifications. I got a good job. I was earning more than my Dad when I was in my twenties. And I wasn't the only one. Lots of the lads I grew up with did well. Lots of them moved away for work. We just seemed to have it better than our parents. And our parents had it better than their parents. That's the way it's supposed to be, isn't it? Things are supposed to get better. Your kids should be doing better than you did. But then I don't think that's the way it is now. I can't say kids today have it better than we did... They might get better wages, but they've lost buying power. We could buy houses, holidays, cars. Even people on good wages these days can't buy a house [...]. But there's something else isn't there? I don't know. I think we had a community. My kids didn't really have that, growing up. We knew the neighbours. We'd all walk to school together, me and my pals, a big group of us. I knew where everyone lived. I'm not saying we were one big happy family but, I don't know. Kids today, not just kids, they just don't seem happy. They don't seem to have, I don't know, the support to get on, do you know what I mean? My kids had friends and everything, but it was all, well, it all seemed to be a bit more distant. They had friends at school, and one or two who lived close by. But I wanted them to enjoy all that like I enjoyed it'.

'I think we don't know where we're going. I think, as a nation, we're lost. There's no clear plan. We can't build anything now. All the big industries have shut down. We don't even make our own steel anymore. The future seems, well, messy and a bit grey, I guess I'd say. I don't know where we're going, and I think if you'd asked me ten, twenty years ago I would've said different. I mean, I think my generation have really messed things up. The future doesn't look good, and if I really think about it, I can't see any way that's going to change. No cause for optimism. That's my depressing conclusion'.

Graham is 49. He is divorced and has a 15-year-old daughter. He works as a delivery driver for a large super-market and lives in a small flat close to the centre of town.

'I've had so many jobs these last ten, fifteen years. I worked in a call centre for a while, that was the worst. I prefer the driving because I can get out and about. I hated being sat in an office. Where I work now, it's a bit more relaxed in some ways. I can get out and away from it all. But the money: I mean, I've got nowt, really. I'd like to get out for a pint with the lads, but, well, it's difficult. I have to budget for everything now. Plan ahead. I don't complain. I've got my own place, Netflix, and as you can see, I'm not going hungry!'

Graham's daughter has a neurological condition that has slowed her development and affected her schooling:

'The whole thing we've gone through with Clare has been a massive learning experience. For years we were scrambling around, try to find out what's wrong. That whole thing took its toll. But at least now we know. We've got a name for it. We got some help from the doctors, but there's nothing at the school. And Clare's not the only one. There's loads of kids there with problems. It's like there's an epidemic of kids suffering with these conditions. There's so many kids with problems. They need help, proper focused help, but they get fuck all as far as I can tell'.

'Every now and then it'll hit me. Look at me. I'm not healthy. Her mother's not neither. Who is going to watch out for her when we're gone? My family's scattered about now. Everyone's got their own stuff going on. And [my ex-wife's] family, her parents are gone, her brothers are useless. That's what I've discovered, getting older. No one cares. People talk a good game, but most people won't get off their arses to help you out. The hours we've spent trying to get help for Clare. People just don't care. If they have to do something, they can't be bothered. If there was ever a community in this town, it's gone. Totally gone. What you've got is a make-believe community. I will see neighbours now, people I've known for years, and we will say hello, a little joke, and that's it. Most of them wouldn't piss on me if I was on fire. It's like that at work. I'll deliver to old people, and they just want you to have a bit of crack with them. I'll give them a bit of banter, make them smile, it's not the hardest thing in the world, is it? But even that's asking too much for some people'.

'I think there was a community once. I think I grew up in a real community, or at least the tail end of one. I'm not saying it was perfect, but there wasn't as many selfish cunts about, only bothered about money, only bothered about themselves. When I look back, I grew up with some properly kind people, you know? Family and friends. But now what have you got? And I think it's all affected me. Just seeing what people are. That you're basically on your own. I don't know how to say it. Just the coldness of it. It affected me. It's like, you wanted it to be one way, but it turned out to be the other. We are just dying out, aren't we?'

'I don't blame the politicians. I blame the people... The politicians are just selfish and useless like everyone else. Why wouldn't you expect a politician to be a lying bastard these days? What, you expect them to actually be good people, caring, trying to help people? Those days are long gone. So, I've just come to accept it. I have some proper good friends and I'm lucky to have them. I've got my daughter, who's perfect. That's what I've got. The rest of it, you can keep. What's the opposite of progress? That's what happened to this country: the opposite of progress'.

Anne is 51. She was in the same year at school as Arthur, who was quoted above. She is married and lives in a well-kept three-bedroom terraced house just around the corner from her old school. She works for a large supermarket chain. She has one daughter, who recently graduated from university.

'There's a sadness, isn't there? It's quite depressing, I think. You don't see anyone with a smile on their face, now. People are struggling. There just seems to be much less money about. And less positivity. I try to be positive every day. I will smile and try and have a bit of a laugh at work. But if I'm honest, I can't be positive about the future. I'm not sure why. Joanne [Anne's daughter] will be OK, but she will have to move, won't she, to get a decent job. Lots of people have moved for work. So many people have left, people my age. And then you've got strangers around, and you've got to start from scratch making friends. There's just that sense that things are going to get worse. We used to have foreign holidays. Spain, Portugal, Tenerife we went to a couple of times. But not now. We used to plan, where shall we go? I used to look forward to a bit of sun. I miss that a bit, you know? Not just the holiday, the looking forward bit of it'.

'I don't really know about politics. I've never been interested in all of that. I've voted, but I can't see the point now. They all just seem the same to me. If I try to say it, what I want is someone to change things, to bring back that positivity, but there isn't anybody, is there? I just block it out if I hear someone talking about politics now [...]. It would be great if we could get somebody who really could do something, something for the better, but what's the point in all that? They can't do it. They can't do anything. And it's going in the opposite direction. I just think lots of people have given up hope.... [My family] just make the best of things. Try and be happy. See friends. We've got Christmas coming up. There's no sense in waiting for that lot [politicians] to help us'.

'If I look into the far, far future, when I'm gone, I don't think there'll be anyone from my family around here. Joanne [Anne's daughter] will move away. There'll be no ties to this place, and that makes me a bit sad [...]. Just because, I think of my Mam, and her Mam. We were here, weren't we? We lived our lives here. It's just a bit sad, thinking about it like that. Everything that ever happened to me happened here. Think of all those different generations, the weddings, the funerals, the christenings, it all happened in this place here. And there's so many good memories. And then, we'll be gone, like we've left everything behind, like it's all forgotten. I don't like to think of it all being forgotten'.

'I think when Joanne has kids, she will push them with the education. I think they will be, I don't know, down south somewhere I suppose. If you've got education, you've got a chance. But I think, this place, they'll just leave it to get worse. There's nothing anyone can do. I think people put themselves first now, so there's nothing there to really build on. No one wants to deal with it. No one wants to deal with the problems'.

Anne clearly feels tied to previous generations of her family who lived similar lives in this place. For her, to abandon the town of her birth is to cast aside the ties that bind her to past generations. While she does not express it directly, she seems to feel the weight of expectation, as if generations gone by are somehow looking to her to ensure the continuity of the family in this specific locale. To leave this place would be an act of erasure, as if those past generations had been cut free from their moorings and left to float away into the nothingness of unremembered history. But the saddest aspect of Anne's testimony is that, while she accepts the burden of maintaining her family's bonds to this specific locale and its culture, she also appears to accept that she will fail in this task. Current generations will leave, and nothing will be left behind. Mindful that to stay is to accept that one's life will be shaped by continued socio-economic decline and community decomposition, Anne endorses her daughter's decision move away. Her daughter and subsequent generations will move elsewhere in an effort to remain attached to the social and economic mainstream, and it makes little sense to criticise them for doing so.

Anne clearly wants to keep the flame of affective remembrance alive, but she accepts that she cannot. The flame will be extinguished, and all she will have to sustain herself will be an increasingly distant relationship with a daughter absorbed in other matters, a meagre income and her own unique assortment of memories of a vital and vivid world that could have elevated the lives of countless generations to come. When Anne finally succumbs, the chain will be broken. The light of affective remembrance will be fully extinguished. Scarcely any evidence will remain that Anne and countless generations of her family were ever here.

3

LOST ROOTS

This chapter uses interview data to identify and develop a number of key themes that emerged from the study. It focuses, in particular, on the people, places and times that so often structure the nostalgic memories of the participants. Anne, who we discussed at length in the last chapter, was lucky enough to have retained what seemed to be a range of clear memories of her early life and the loved ones that made it such a happy time for her. She comments thus:

'I have good memories of my Mam. I can still see her face, when I think back. She was dead nine years in August. She was a great mam. She was a lot of fun, especially before when we were younger. She was ill a long time and there's memories there too. I remember her singing. I think of that every now and then. I'm in my school uniform, just in from school I think, because she's in the kitchen cooking. She's singing. She liked all those old-time songs. She made a good life for us. It was a happy house'.

Not all interviewees benefitted from a happy childhood. Doug is 49 years old. He works part-time delivering takeaway food. Partially reliant upon benefits, he now lives in a tiny one-bedroom flat in what is perhaps the city's most ethnically and religiously diverse neighbourhood. While his present accommodation is far from perfect, he is happy to have moved from his last residence, an even smaller bedsit, which was burgled twice in the space of a week. He has a 24-year-old daughter but doesn't see her very often:

'I think back to those days more and more. I didn't have the greatest of times as a kid. My mam was difficult. There was always arguing and shouting. My Dad, I don't think I ever got to know him really. But that's the thing: I can remember the difficult stuff, but it doesn't bother me anymore. It did, but not anymore. And there's good stuff in there too. I remember Phil [Doug's elder brother] and how he was. He helped me in a lot of ways. He really tried to look after me, growing up. And I've still got old friends back from when I was a boy. We've stuck together for a lot of years, and I like that. When we get together, we'll always go through the old stories. Daft stuff we used to get up to, times when we had a good laugh. Sometimes I'll catch myself laughing at memories of, well, just us being out and about when we were young. It's nice. It cheers me up. I'll be off doing something, and a memory will pop into my head, and I'll have a little laugh to myself, you know?'

Doug split up from his long-term partner nine years ago.

'I think of the what-might-have-beens, you know, if this hadn't have happened, if that hadn't have happened. I went off the rails there for a bit. There was a lot of stuff going on, and it was just a difficult time really. Phil died, obviously, and that knocked me for six. I didn't think it did at the time, but it definitely did, looking back. I think about that a lot. Bad decisions I made. But it's all part of getting older, isn't it? You think back more. Good times and bad times. I'm more positive these days, but that's just because I've got used to it; I've learnt to accept things. I don't want to live in the past, but, for me, I don't see the bad times as all that bad anymore. And the good times were, you know, great times if I really think about it'.

'It feels like my life has shrunk down a lot. I don't see as many people, and I just like to keep myself to myself. The people I knew when I was younger, a lot have just gone, who knows where. I'm not a part of all that anymore. I try not to go back [to my old neighbourhood]. It's not the same. I don't know anyone there anymore, and it just feels a bit weird [. . .]. Like everything's the same but everything's different at the same time. I'm just happy in my own little space. Trying to stay healthy is the thing now. I don't look to the future much. I try not to think about it, I suppose. I used to years ago, but I've kind of let it go know. Whatever happens, happens. I can't control it. But, yes, I do drift off with the memories a lot more. I replay stuff in my head, mostly the good things now. I think about the happy times and try to stay positive. If I think too much about now, I'll go off the rails again. There's too much sadness there, really. That's why I drift off with the memories. It's an escape when you remember the better stuff'.

Parents inspired a great deal of positive reflection, but people were often nostalgic for siblings and friends with whom they had lost touch. Keith is 56 years old. He works for a large manufacturer:

'I have this memory of an old pal of mine, Mike. He moved away, ages ago. I haven't seen him in like, twenty-odd years. He was a proper comedian, he was. He'd have us in stitches. Terrible piss-taker, always out for a laugh. Anyway, he'd just go off on one and make up these daft stories. Stuff like, he ran into the Queen coming out of the chippy, or he'd been working at Rod Stewart's house fitting a new shitter, or he pulled a supermodel queuing at the dole, that kind of thing, do you know what I mean? I remember, clear as day, here's Mike doing one of his stories, and everyone's laughing. We're sat in the [pub], and everyone is just pissing themselves. I remember,

I'm sat at a table, and there's about ten full pints on the table. I remember that clearly. Like ten, twelve pints of lager on the table, and the sun's coming in through the window. I don't remember the story or anything like that. I just remember the laughing. Why do I remember that, eh? What's that about? [...] Yes, I suppose. It's about being happy. I was maybe at my happiest then. Young, no responsibilities, just having a laugh with the lads'.

'Everybody's nostalgic for when they were young. I used to get that with my Mam. She'd be just sitting, thinking, and I always used to be like, what's she doing? She'd say she was off in her memories. Thinking about her Dad a lot, times when she was a girl, stuff like that. She did it more and more towards the end there, and sometimes she'd get confused, calling people by wrong names, stuff like that. She used to say, it goes by so quick, and she was bang on the money there, wasn't she?'

'I think at my age you drift off [into memory] more and more. I'm lucky I've got so many good memories. I don't want to lose that. I think about being out with the lads when I was a young one. It was like one big adventure, that's what I used to think. And that's what I remember most from that time: laughing. Just, great times. Before I got married, before the responsibilities and the work and the house and bills and all of that. It was just a brighter time, all of it. You don't appreciate it until it's gone. I wish I'd made the most of it. I enjoyed it, but I wish I could've enjoyed it more'.

'I've got memories of when the kids were young. Holidays, things like that, times when everyone's smiling. I like to think of them with their Nana, like her reading to them when they were tiny. I've got this memory of us at the beach. I'm chasing a ball, but the wind's got it and every time I get close it blows away again. The kids were howling. I've got memories of school, but they're hazy now. They don't come to me as often as they used to. I can remember some of the teachers, messing about at school dinners, things like that. I've got memories of walking to school through the park with the lads. Some random bit and pieces pop into my head now and then. I remember the old science rooms with the Bunsen burners, do you remember them? I was thinking about that just the other day: Some kid singeing his hair and everyone pissing themselves laughing. I remember walking from the school to the church for Christmas carols. I think of that every Christmas. It's a nice memory. Christmas is great when you're that age. You can see the end of school and the start of the [Christmas] holidays. Everyone's happy, even the teachers'.

'I have good memories about my Dad. I remember him sat in front of the telly reading the paper in his overalls. He loved the football. He'd come and watch us play when we had a game on the playing fields down the bottom there. I took him to the match once, when he was older. He didn't say anything really, but I could tell he loved it, the stadium and the crowd and floodlights and everything. We walked home, all the way. It was freezing cold. When we got in my Mam was really happy, the two of us out together'.

Greg is 49. He is the co-owner of a small building business:

'My Mam was the greatest. Just amazing, what she did. Two boys, all by herself. We were tearaways, the two of us. Not bad lads, but just, always up to something. In trouble at school. But she was great. She was a dinner lady. She'd do bits of cleaning. But happy with it. We were always, like, super clean, clean clothes. That's stuck with me, that has. And we always had enough. We didn't do without anything, really. That's what we thought. We had new trainers, which was a big thing at the time. There were always birthday presents, Christmas presents. We had a great time, as kids. All my memories are happy. It was a great time to be alive, I think, a great time to grow up. It's difficult to remember one thing, but

I can picture her in the house. She'd be cleaning, cooking, ironing, whatever, smiling. I remember us all sat in front of the telly, laughing at whatever was on'.

Mac is 54. He works for a large multinational manufacturing company. However, when we spoke he was on long-term sick leave after suffering serious heart problems.

'We were working class I suppose you'd say. We grew up here and we were the same as everyone else, really. I supposed, looking back, it was a tough place, but we didn't care. It all just seemed normal. And we had good people around us. We had cousins, aunts and uncles close by. We were brought up respectful. There was always people around watching what you were up to [...]. We were never rich, but we had a car, holidays, there was money for what we needed. And we grew up expecting to live like that. Everyone was big on work, and I did OK work wise. The kids grew up with nice things. We've had holidays all over the place. I've been thinking about it more, with the heart problems. There's a pinch obviously, with the sick pay, and we got hammered with the inflation. The mortgage has gone right up, and I can't wait to be rid of it. But with the health, now I'm thinking, what if I can't go back [to work]? What if I get a bad one [a heart attack]? How's everyone going to manage? The kids still need us, just for everything really. The wife's job doesn't pay much. I get that worry that I didn't do enough, like I've fucked things up somehow. Like I should've been saving, I should've been earning more, I should've moved jobs maybe, we should've sold the house and got somewhere smaller. I don't want to let anyone down. It's a nagging feeling really. It's not just the money. Things are going to get harder and they're going to struggle. Lots of people are'.

Darren is 51 and works in a warehouse:

'When I was young, I wasn't bothered. It's that confidence, when you're young. I didn't think anything could bother me.

I'd always be able to get a job, I'd always have money. If I wanted something, I could get it. It didn't matter. It's that confidence, like it'll all work out fine; there's no need to worry, do you know what I mean? That goes when you get older. I mean, I always did alright, do you know what I mean? I worked, I spent my money, and it was all fine. I didn't, you know, plan things out much because there wasn't any need to. You think there's always going to be a job there for you and you don't need to think about it. Then you've got kids; I think that's when it changes. You worry for your kids. Now I'm thinking I should've planned it better. And they're going to have problems, I can just feel it. Things aren't going to go as well for them... I just don't think they're prepared for it, the toughness of the world. I mean, bless them, they're nice, kind kids, but what'll happen when something bad happens? They're ten times cleverer than me, but they're a bit innocent. You want them to have what it takes to just cope with stuff, the bad stuff that comes along. Now I've got, what about the mortgage, what about this bill, that bill? I worry about, what if they lose their jobs, what if they can't sort this out, that out? What ifs, all the time. And we've got less spare now. It just goes. I used to be able to spend, like money wasn't a problem. It's a weird, weird thing. All of that has just disappeared, that confidence. You try to put a brave face on, but I can't help them now. You want to protect them, but you can't'.

Dexter is 53. After a peripatetic youth and a series of short-lived careers, he is now back living in his hometown working as a self-employed labourer. He has lost touch with his eldest daughter, but he is now in regular contact with his other two children:

'If I look back, what I think is it was all a bit more relaxed. I didn't have the stresses. I can remember I was into designer clothes. Christ, the money I spent. Going out, girlfriends, holidays. I thought life is going to be easy. Life was just life, and you just got on with it; you didn't have to think things through. But things you could rely on, it turns out you couldn't rely on. I never thought I'd struggle like I have. I didn't plan for it. It all just seemed to happen so quick. Like, you're doing fine and then, bang, you're right in the shit. No warning, no nothing. It's like feeling old. I was expecting it to be gradual, but I realised it's already gone, and it's already done. You're thinking, "fuck me, where did the time go?". You're an old fart talking about the good old days, remembering back to when you were a lad'.

'You can't rely on anything now. People had jobs that paid when I was young. You could get a good job and stick with it. Loads of people around here pushed on. They got jobs, got money, got on with living. I don't understand it now. Things seem to be going the other way. I remember the pubs were busy all the time. Music playing, people laughing. It was a great time to be young. Now, you think, that's it gone. Downhill from here'.

Dougie is 54 and works in a factory:

'People like me can't get ahead today. You work every hour that God sends, you'll still end up with nowt. I used to think, those people on benefits: why? Why would you live like that? Work is great, you can have a laugh, you get money, and you can treat yourself. Now, I don't know. I work like a dog. I'm knackered all the time. I've worked hard all my life. What have I got? I feel old before my time, I suppose. I thought I'd have longer'.

We met Paul in the last chapter. He has a mid-level sales position in a large retail group. He has this to say about the changes in the workplace:

'I liked it when I started there. I was getting good money, and I just liked the action of the job. It's nice to be good at something, the hours go by quicker. But now, all the fun's gone out of it. I feel old. All these young kids have come in.

There's no banter. It's all, well, much more serious. And much more competitive. There's so much arse-kissing and trying to get ahead. It wasn't like that before. I can see people fucking each other over, and that's just a normal part of it now [...]. I'm old fashioned, I suppose. And it never stops. The job is basically the same, but everything else around it has changed massively. I can't get my head around it. And I've stopped trying, I know I have. The days are longer and everything's a pain because the fun's gone out of it. Training for this, training for that. I don't understand most of it. They just go on and on about stuff that's got nothing to do with the job. I've just learnt to button my lip and keep my head down. But any minute now they'll be calling me into the office and asking me if it's not time for me to do something else. That's how they do it. Out with the old, in with the new. Get someone else in who knows the lingo. Someone who knows how to play the game. Maybe I should see it as a positive. But it's just starting from scratch, starting the bottom. At my age. And the other places I could go will just be the same. I'm just clinging on, hoping they'll forget about me. If I can cling on five more years, just 'til the boys are set up, that'll do for me'.

The expectation of decline, and a general belief that the past offered more to ordinary people, can be identified in every facet of the data gathered during this project. The assumption often seemed to be that the problems of the present would proliferate, worsen and diversify. Consequently, the future – for them, and those they loved – would be qualitatively worse than the present and absent of the things they valued about the past. For participants, the future seemed vague and featureless, save for the assumption that they would be poorer, more isolated, and less able to cope with the rapidly evolving demands of mainstream social and economic life.

Beneath surface descriptions of their disorderly worlds lies an obdurate sense of rootlessness. They can access in memory a reasonably stable sense of home. They once felt comfortable and secure in their home environments. They formed part of a community that enjoyed the depth and uniqueness of its culture. But now, all of that seemed to have disappeared. They couldn't identify it anywhere in the present, and so they assumed it couldn't exist in the future. Participants also often seemed anxious that their rootless children now have nothing to hold them in place as they prepare to be endlessly buffeted by the coming storms. Every now and then, participants' assessments of change seemed to be informed by a degree of guilt, as if they were personally responsible for failing to equip their children with whatever it was that might've allowed them to meet coming challenges with confidence. Other participants externalised these sentiments, blaming vaguely composed external others for stripping them of what were once taken for granted forms of security and the pleasures of a supportive community life. However, in a majority of cases, participants seemed untroubled by guilt and disinclined to blame others for the negative changes that had disturbed the coherence and stability of their lives. The changes we discussed were, it seemed, too vast and too all-encompassing to be fully comprehended. The most common response to these changes was befuddlement and a general estrangement from a world that seemed to make little sense. However, as we talked and a greater degree of clarity emerged, it was common for befuddlement to morph into anger or sadness.

Simone Weil's *The Need for Roots* was published posthumously just after the end of the Second World War.[1] Centring on absence and what we need to live a rewarding life, it offers a preceptive reading of the social malaise that Weil believed had disrupted European civilisation during the first third of the 20th century. Weil claimed that industrialisation, war and the gradual erosion of established social structures had 'uprooted' people from their cultures and communities.

The people increasingly felt distant from tradition and traditional morality, the intimacies of communal life and long-standing cultural and ethical obligations to one another.

This growing sense of detachment had led to a loss of meaning. People felt adrift. They needed order. They needed to accept moral authority and the rights of all people to human dignity. They needed shared goals and projects and compelling visions of a better future. All should be able to access and benefit from collectively owned goods. The public realm must be shaped by an abiding commitment to honesty, integrity and the well-being of the collective. The people needed to feel a degree of duty to others and a degree of responsibility for their welfare. They needed to feel secure, safe and financially stable and free to fully express themselves without fear of retribution. They also needed to feel connected to their historical and cultural roots and the places where these roots were most meaningful.

Without roots, the core requirements of a fulfilling and meaningful life were forever out of reach. Without roots, true communities would fall apart. The glue that bonded individuals together and encouraged them to acknowledge shared interests and live by shared rules would lose its power to adhere and the people would drift off to live monadic and ultimately unsatisfying lives. Societies would become more unstable and the lives of the people gradually more unhappy, unfulfilling and insecure. For Weil, it was vital that we take on the fight to preserve our roots.

Many readers today might immediately assume that Weil was a social and political conservative, committed to preserving the exclusivity of white, western patriarchal societies while ignoring the myriad injustices that litter their history. But that isn't the case at all. Weil was concerned principally with the plight of the poor, and her intellectual commitments are broadly split between Christian ethics, mysticism and a philosophical concern with the effects of absence and loss. Of course, Weil's thesis might be seen as essentially conservative today because we are living through an era of compulsory but insubstantial liberalism, an unanchored late liberalism increasingly devoid of the basic characteristics of liberalism itself. While Weil was keen to preserve traditional communities, the tendency these days is to imagine traditional communities to be aggressively hostile to non-members and those who do not immediately conform to communal norms.

Just as neoliberalism established itself as hegemonic in the fields of politics and economics, cosmopolitanism managed to subtly fashion a hegemonic position in our cultural and intellectual life. As we have seen, to speak against the free movement of labour and capital across borders is to invite allegations of racism and ignorance. Identifying the economic, environmental and geopolitical processes that underpin so much migration today is considered an unwelcome distraction from our ethical duty to immediately welcome migrants and revel in surface level diversity and perpetual change. We are encouraged to form the view that our communities must be open, diverse and subject to constant democratic change rather than beholden to dead traditions and the myopic rules they inspire.[2]

Weil suggested rootedness enables people to develop a sense of meaning and nourishing connections to others. This does not mean that we must fight to ensure that the ethnic or religious characteristics of our cultures remain unchanged. Rather, we must extend rights and respect to those who seek admittance to our culture in the expectation that they will reciprocate, accept the history and logic of the culture, conform to its rules and join with their new neighbours in living meaningful lives of peaceful coexistence. Their arrival, of course, then feeds into the history of the culture. Its narratives evolve as it seeks to represent itself to future generations. However, today it often seems that to talk of the benefits of rootedness is to accept a paralysing stuckness that runs contrary to the normative principle that we should see constant change as essential to freedom. Is it reactionary to give primacy to rootedness over movement, to traditional culture over constant cultural innovation, to obligation and the moral life over the pursuit of our own instrumental interests and desires? Is it unethical to give precedence to our own communities, spaces and cultures rather than embrace the vague promise that at some point in the future innovative and inclusive hybrid cultures will magically emerge from global consumer culture to give new meaning to uprooted lives?

The symbolic substance of community life tends to be venerated and passed like a Maussian gift from one generation to the next.[3] This has always been the case.[4] It is not solely a characteristic of white European communities. These gifts can be enjoyed, but they must also be protected and retained so they can be again passed on to the generation that follows. In passing these gifts from one generation to the next, communities remain vital and alive. But there is of course a degree of seriousness and solemnity to this process. Each generation carries the burden of ensuring that the symbolic life of the community can be passed safely on to the next generation. And with each generation, the burden becomes heavier because each generation must also carry the expectations of all preceding generations. It is inevitable that each generation experiences a degree of anxiety that they will be the ones who finally fail to secure the community's continuity, and inevitable that some communities are willing to fight hard to stay true to their sacred task.

In *The Human Condition*, Hannah Arendt argued that we inevitably strive for permanence in a world increasingly characterised by high-paced change.[5] We also need to maintain a sense of familiarity with our environments, our social roles and the core features of our everyday lives. Without a clear sense of rootedness in our experience of labour, work and action, we lose key elements of our humanity. And without familiarity, there can be no sense of home. Our traditions aid our sense of permanence, and our cultures, if working optimally, should host a constant dialogue with the past that enables individuals to identify a degree of continuity and situate themselves in space and time. Like Weil, Arendt believed that mass society, with its emphasis on disposability and its growing antagonism to everything that once seemed fixed and durable, was eroding the sense of permanence and continuity we need to feel fully at home in our world. Slowly, the things we needed to remain fully human were falling away.

The data from this study certainly suggest that people have been alienated from their traditions and cultures and disembedded from their communal spaces they once called home. They increasingly feel themselves to be absent of the forms of support, security and validation they once received. They feel themselves drifting apart from others, increasingly insecure, lost and anxious about the future. They long for the clarity of established meaning and the consolations of vibrant community life. They mourn a lost world in which so much could be taken for granted. They miss its universally accepted rules, meanings and symbols.

Participants often seemed to have come to terms with their own creeping irrelevance. They had grown accustomed to being unrepresented and politically ignored. While they often wanted to cling on as long as possible, they seemed to accept that their skills and their practical role in the economy would soon be at an end. They felt themselves now to be on the outside looking in at environments that were once replete with the real and imagined comforts of home. Certainly, they do not imagine themselves to have been liberated by the process of uprooting. They do not feel themselves to have taken control of their own identities and biographies, and they do not believe themselves able to dedicate what remains of their lives to pursuing their own ephemeral desires. And nor did they believe themselves to be racist for wanting to maintain some semblance of cultural continuity. In the next chapter, we begin to investigate the various forces that uprooted research participants from their communities and histories, leaving them feeling increasingly adrift in a turbulent world that makes precious little sense to them.

4

BEYOND MODERNISM

The rise and diffusion of postmodernism has subtly encouraged the prevailing sense of disorientation and rootlessness that drives so many of us to search for the comforts that seem to lie somewhere within nostalgia's strange confines. At the very centre of postmodernism was the drive to free the people from the iron cage of their own beliefs. Postmodernists suggested modern institutions corralled and contained human experience in the name of repressive orderliness and unthinking social reproduction.[1] We were trapped by strange rules that, when subject to critical interrogation, seemed to be based on nothing more robust than myth, folklore and blind obedience to convention. The masses were shepherded along a narrow path of acceptable behaviour and denied the opportunity to roam. Laws, formal and informal, enforced conventionality and denied the people creative control of their own lives.

For many, post-war social democracy had brought significant material improvements and appeared to offer a framework for the gradual expansion of human freedoms. However, the postmodernists saw the opposite. They believed the people were more repressed than ever. The state and its various institutions had developed new techniques to enforce conventionality. The welfare state seemed to encroach ever more forcefully upon their privacy and independence. Suggestions of progress hid new and more complex strategies to enforce prejudice and sustain the prevailing climate of multi-layered 'unfreedom'. The people lived repressed and cocooned lives, fearful of non-existent gods, the moral judgement of the herd, and the clumsy interventions of the state.

The postmodernists were keen to burst free from the intellectual straitjacket they imagined had been placed upon them by established elites. They hoped to think beyond convention. Pursuant of this goal, they ignored the standard invocation to build a new intellectual edifice that might draw attention and attract support. Their approach would be different. Rather than building something new, they would break apart all existing frameworks of meaning. And so began the project of ceaseless deconstruction. Many postmodernists seemed confident that perpetual deconstruction would reveal the errors, biases and unfounded assumptions present in all aspects of established human knowledge. Relieved of these impediments, an insubstantial and apparently natural freedom would emerge. We would believe in nothing, and amid the nothingness we would be free.

It is often assumed that the postmodernists placed great emphasis on destabilising and deconstructing established structures of knowledge because they were sceptics keen to discard out of date and ossified intellectual conventions so that new and better forms of knowledge could take their place. But this assumption is misguided. Deconstruction was a project without end. Postmodernism was rooted in bleak cynicism rather than healthy scepticism. Ultimately, the post-modernists did not hope to convince the people to stop believing in established forms of knowledge. Nor did they hope to convince the people to start believing in new and better knowledge systems. Rather, when all was said and done, they wanted the people to simply stop believing. Beyond the realm of immediate bodily experience, there existed nothing worthy of belief.

It is also a mistake to assume that postmodernism was a leftist project. It was not. It was, and still is, an outgrowth of philosophical libertarianism. It grew in the shadow of French existentialism and was clearly influenced by the post-structuralism that developed alongside it. On occasion, it borrowed sparingly from phenomenology. However, what was borrowed from phenomenology was pushed in a libertarian direction. Key figures were overtly antagonistic to the growth of post-war welfare state, and their criticism tended to be condemnatory rather than practical and geared towards improvement. Bureaucracies were an impediment to human freedom. The small benefits received by the people were given in exchange for subservience to the obtuse rules that were slowly expanding to encompass every facet of life.

The raw freedom the postmodernists seemed to desire was the abject freedom of total separation and independence. They seemed to aspire to a post-social world absent of authority, rules and obligations to others. Individuals should be entirely unconstrained and free to follow their desires, wherever they may lead. It should come as no surprise to learn that, as the 1980s approached, many postmodernists were attracted by the possibilities of the incipient neoliberalism.

The politics of the postmodernists were decidedly anti-establishment, and so we might reasonably forgive an impartial observer for placing them on the left of the political spectrum. However, we can forgive this mistake because the intellectual left had by this stage been moving in a libertarian direction for quite some time. To the postmodernists, all power was illegitimate. All hierarchies were unjust. To classify postmodernists as leftists perpetuates the longstanding tradition of confusing socialism with progressive liberalism and the proclamations of credentialised liberal activists with the authentic voice of the people. As time passed, the traditional goals of socialism were discarded. The evolving goals of progressive liberalism took their place.

For the postmodernists – as with all liberals and libertarians – the central focus was freedom. They were not concerned with the material interests of the working class. When they did address inequality and material hardship, they were mostly concerned with the effects of these things rather than their causes and then only when they judged the fundamental effect to be a reduction in freedom. Poverty restricted freedom, and therefore poverty should be condemned. But there was no attempt to extend leftist knowledge of capitalism's economic system, and no attempt to develop a politics that placed the injustices of the economic realm centrally in analyses of the post-war world.

Their politics also had a clear 'activist' orientation. In keeping with the fundaments of their intellectual approach, there was no identifiable programme for renewal. They were, of course, against those things that seemed to restrict human freedom. In the hope of freeing the people, they hoped to dispense with, or at least ruthlessly strip back, every bureaucracy and institution that seemed to support tradition, religion and cultural convention. But what seemed to be the positive aspect of their politics rested on the removal of a negative. They had no obvious programme to put in place that would increase human freedom, save for the fact that they would take away those things they believed restricted human freedom. As the neoliberal era began to take shape, this mode of negative politics would subsume political debate, merging with the toxic assumption that structural change was unnecessary and the inevitable road to totalitarianism.

There wasn't a scintilla of socialism in postmodernism. Despite clinging on to their carefully orchestrated image as radicals, some leading lights dismissed socialism as an anachronism. It was incapable of pivoting and refocusing its critique upon the forms of injustice the postmodernists believed to be synonymous with the times. The left had to be transformed. It had to leave behind socialism and materialism. It had to stop obsessing about capitalism and economic injustice and direct its critique at the diverse forces that curtailed human experience.

Postmodernism certainly seemed to offer a radical break from existing paradigms. However, the radical break it offered was in many respects stylistic rather than substantive. Although the ideas it sought to radically extend were already in circulation, it somehow managed to retain an image of audacious novelty, which was nicely complemented by the haughty self-assurance that seems proper to French intellectual life. Many of its most esteemed thinkers were as bluntly dismissive of the great figures of western thought as they were of the restrictive orthodoxies of western grammar and syntax.[2] But there was little interest in capitalism or the effects of economic necessity upon our cultural and private lives. Nor did they hold out much hope for capitalism's alternatives. For the most part, the postmodernists saw only totalitarian oppression in really existing communism, and socialism seemed fetishistically invested in the construction of sprawling bureaucracies and intrusive agencies keen to stamp out the flower of freedom wherever it bloomed. For them, the standard ideological jousting between capitalism and communism held no interest whatsoever. The old, outmoded obsession with revolution studiously avoided the true locus of political contestation. What the postmodernists proposed was a cultural revolution, a revolution of the self and the spirit, a deconstructive 'revolution' that could take place without disturbing the structures of western capitalism.

Postmodernism merged with other elements of 'the cultural turn', catalysing the liberal counterculture that had gathered pace during the 60s. Of course, the call to disempower institutions, dispense with cultural conventions and free the individual from unthinking subservience to the structures of gendered biographical predestination could already be heard loud and clear across the intellectual landscape before postmodernism really began to stretch its legs during the 1970s. It is difficult to identify precisely what postmodernism contributed to the counterculture other than to encourage key protagonists to press the accelerator of cultural change firmly to the floor. The orthodoxies of the modern age were not simply out-of-date and in need to renovation; they were oppressive and inhuman. Lives were being wasted in mindless subservience to a multitude of repressive norms and atavistically productive discourses. Deciding to ignore social and cultural rules took bravery and may necessitate some sacrifices, but a purer freedom was available to those who could brave the storm.

Postmodernism tacitly spurred the libertarianism of Western intellectual life. Its anti-establishment ethos challenged canonical knowledge and the basic precepts commonly used to know the world. Disciplines across the humanities and social sciences became increasingly dominated by liberal critiques of power, convention, morality and justice. Beneath such critique lay a range of assumptions about the nature of freedom, human subjectivity and the will of the people. When investigated with care, these assumptions revealed the close ideological connections between the liberal left and the liberal right. Despite the growing tendency to denigrate, mock and grossly misrepresent the claims of one's ideological opponents, the heated rhetorical sparring between the liberal left and the liberal right seemed increasingly staged and structured to ensure that fundamental issues which loomed large in popular experience of everyday life remained unexamined.

Very often, the liberal left was as opposed to the state's interventions as the liberal right. Both wings of this post-political liberal alliance agreed upon the primacy of freedom and, as the 20th century progressed, both tended to favour a negative account of freedom. The fight for freedom involved disempowering external forces that held authority over the individual, or otherwise shaped the individual's choices and behaviour. It did not involve giving individuals the basic tools they needed to fashion their own freedom. And, of course, both groups tended to thoughtlessly reproduce the standard claim that the people wanted this threadbare negative freedom above all else. The liberal right claimed the people wanted to be free from the clumsy incursions of the state and the unjust burden of taxation so they might enjoy greater opportunities to choose. The liberal left tended to offer a more detailed exposition of the various structures that impeded human experience, but at no point did their demand for cultural freedom clash with the liberal right's demand for economic freedom.

Postmodernism did not greatly clash with many established features of the left's political culture. Progressive liberalism has been a noteworthy characteristic of leftist discourse since the 19th century.[3] As time passed, it displaced the material and representational concerns of the working classes to become the dominant ideological feature of the left's famously broad church. Slowly but surely, popular opinion of left politics changed. Where once the left had seemed dominated by the aesthetics of the industrial working class and principally concerned with practical demands for greater material security, increasingly the left seemed to have taken on the aesthetics of the counterculture and was characterised by fragmented politics of student radicalism and cause-based activism. By the time postmodernism became influential, to be on the left was to be liberal on all social and cultural issues, and the core strategy of the liberal left seemed to involve little more than attempting to shame power into granting a few minor cultural reforms while muttering a few muted calls to address economic injustice.

The post-sixties left offered no substantive alternatives. Large expanses of the left gave up the traditional hope of actually taking power and using it to create a more equitable world. For them, power tended to corrupt. It was better to take up a lofty position of permanent critique divorced from the grubby business of practical class politics. From this position, they could establish the left as the voice of pure ethics, shaping political discussion, influencing public opinion and shaming powerholders by revealing their procession of inevitable interventionist failures.[4]

This reformed left was incapable of offering any note-worthy opposition to the strident neoliberalism that estab-lished itself as economic common sense during the 1980s. What opposition it could muster was offered by the remnants of the traditional left, a tired old warrior tilting at windmills as it championed the material interests of the people. Out-numbered, outgunned, and often as despised by the liberal left as they were by the liberal right, the old left could cling on no longer and quietly succumbed, leaving the way open for the left and right-wing variants of neoliberalism to continue normalising austerity, enriching oligarchs and provoking ethno-nationalist reaction while establishing cynicism, anxiety and enmity as core features of everyday life.[5]

This extended discussion of postmodernism serves to encourage the reader to think about the evolution of intel-lectual life during the latter half of the 20th century and how intellectual trends can subtly influence politics, culture and the route we take into the future. Postmodernism was not the only branch of philosophy that prepared the ground for neo-liberalism's ascent. However, it deserves close attention because at its centre lies a forthright critique of the keystones of western civilisation. As I have already said, the cynicism of postmodernism and its domain assumption that there is nothing worthy of belief are often misread as a desire to dispense with the past's intellectual impediments so that we might know the world better. However, despite Foucault's playful historical cherry-picking, there exists little or no positive content in postmodernism. Its only claim to revelatory knowledge centred upon encouraging its audience to accept that what was 'present' in traditional beliefs was prejudiced, illogical and often corrupted by the malign interests of elites.

Beneath their tangled and obtuse prose lay a hidden naturalism. It is difficult to avoid the conclusion that the postmodernists assumed that, once we had dispensed with corrupt knowledge, we would immediately be able to experience the great joys of freedom. Both the repressive and discursively productive fundaments upon which social life is built were presented by postmodernists as freedom-sapping tyrannies. Morality has no logical foundation. Our obligations to others reduce our own sovereign freedom. Our schools, our parents and our communities demand obedience to humdrum conventionality. Our lives become grey as we merge with the herd and live in fear of its judgement.

Throughout the expansive literature on postmodern thought, freedom has no defining qualities and tends to be presented merely as the obverse of tyranny. Dispensing with multiple sources of tyranny, the postmodernists seemed to be saying, will naturally increase human freedom. For the most part, the freedom they advocated was the freedom to pursue desire unhindered. Clumsy attempts to regulate desire were stupid and oppressive. The great problem with this approach, of course, is that they failed to consider the fundamental dialectics of freedom. Desire was, for them, a positive essence that gave colour to life. They displayed little interest in the ancient suggestion that true freedom was dependent upon freedom from desire itself.[6]

Postmodernism did not last, but it really did not need to. Instead, it compelled the collective forces of cultural liberalism to accelerate into the cultural turn rather than slowing down to ensure the whole extended charabanc remained on the road. And yet, remain on the road it did. With its foot pressed firmly to the floor, the new cultural and economic liberalism careened into the future, leaving its one-time competitors obscured by the dust of history.

Before positioning the advent of postmodern neoliberalism more firmly in relation to this study, it behoves us to first acknowledge that cultures and not fixed. All cultures evolve. Despite claims to the contrary, western culture evolved comparatively quickly in the decades that followed the end of the Second World War. The cultural homogeneity that many believed typified the first half of the 20th century simply couldn't hold. A new and more heterogeneous world was beginning to emerge. Ordinary people were becoming more tolerant of otherness. Religious commitment was declining, and the old class system was beginning to loosen up. Modern consumerism was beginning to infiltrate and reform our cultural lives, changing our ambitions and desires and subtly shaping our relationships with others. The prejudices of closed community life were falling apart. Yet many cultural liberals were unwilling to wait around for their preferred changes to fully materialise. They wanted to be free from the shackles of the past as quickly as possible. Perceived structural impediments were not to be deconstructed brick by brick but demolished immediately alongside the bigotries and injustices that sustained them. Once these tyrannies were gone, a clear route to a better future would materialise. Given its relatively short time span compared to the centuries or millennia of self-construction taken by the great religions and modern nations, postmodernism wasn't a patient sculptor's hand; it was a wrecking ball.

The politico-economic vehicle carrying the wrecking ball was a far more substantive piece of kit. The new age of neoliberalism – dreamt since the 1920s and test-driven in the early 1970s by audacious and disruptive banking reforms – began in earnest at the beginning of the 1980s. Neoliberals had waged a dogged campaign to unseat and replace their socialist and social democratic adversaries. Now they pursued an equally forceful battle to ensure they could never return.

They ruthlessly lambasted the mixed economy of post-war social democracy. The state was depicted as sclerotic and incapable of moving with the times. The market was fleet-of-foot, adaptable and dedicated to delivering what customers needed. The sprawling Kafkaesque bureaucracies of the welfare state were nightmarish tyrannies that could no longer be countenanced. The nation needed to be outward facing. It needed to throw itself into the interminable competition of the emerging global marketplace. To succeed, nations needed to be ruthlessly efficient and adaptable. They needed to sever the sentimental ties that prevented them from moving purposefully into the future. Stifling dependencies must be immediately dispensed with. The boundless creativity of the people would be the fuel that would drive the nation to global success. It was a mantra that was issued in virtually every newspaper and on every TV screen by almost all politicians. Most members of the commentariat diligently repeated the standard talking points. It was impossible to argue against the kinds of change proposed by the neoliberals and continue to be given a mainstream platform. After all, to argue against neoliberal change was to argue against positivity, dynamism and the benefits that would inevitably follow. It was to suggest that change wasn't necessary and that we should settle for inefficiency and decline.

For the neoliberals, there was no logical alternative. The nation needed to adapt or die. Failure was inconceivable. The rewards were potentially huge. With their ideological adversaries silenced, the neoliberals' message began to catch on among ordinary people. Social democratic interventionism was gone and could not return. It seemed impossible to pull in the opposite direction. Freed from the dusty clutches of the decrepit state, the market would carry us all to a better future. Everyone seemed to agree. The change inherent to neoliberalism seemed irresistible.

Neoliberalism became a terminus of sorts, an end point from which we need never depart. Neoliberals mistakenly believed they had found a range of policies that would constantly drive the lopsided economic growth they favoured and enable creative entrepreneurs to keep delivering the gadgets, gizmos and hedonistic experiences that gave the newly constituted consumer society its surface vitality.

The mainstream left accepted that the state should be disempowered and concern itself principally with encouraging private capital investment. The state's representatives threw themselves into a prolonged public performance of self-flagellating apology and repentance, talking up the god-like genius of the investment class and talking down the ability of the state to do anything useful for the people. The mainstream left also seemed to accept the central neoliberal claim that the organised working class was an impediment to growth and the smooth functioning of markets.[7] Union membership declined enormously, as did working-class representation at the forefront of most unions. Talk of class and class politics simply disappeared from popular political discussion.

AN END TO HISTORY?

Many noteworthy academics and intellectuals have explored the relationship between neoliberalism and the supposed end of history.[8] Neoliberalism had successfully swept its antagonists from the ideological map. In the absence of comprehensible alternatives, it ceased to operate as an ideology on the field of politics. Instead, politics itself was absorbed into neoliberalism. At election time, the people were free to pick whichever neoliberal party best seemed to represent their interests. If one neoliberal party failed, the public could vote to replace it with another. History appeared to have ended. Chronological time continued to tick by, but all change could be accommodated within the framework of electoral democracy and neoliberal capitalism. The future would be just like the present but with better tech.

The 'end of history' thesis, of course, suggests a degree of stuckness. As neoliberalism continued its journey from the particular to the universal, it became increasingly clear that history had become bogged down and was unable to move productively forward. Most of those who have theorised and analysed this dark period in our history did not suggest that change became impossible or unnecessary.[9] Rather, they problematise this stuckness, identifying the forces that prevent forward motion and the tools that might encourage the engine of history to once again rumble into action.[10]

Despite neoliberalism's many injustices, the people could not dispense with it.[11] It was impossible to vote for a political party that had the wherewithal to actually break free from this stifling consensus and drive history in a more productive direction. However, just as neoliberalism seemed to remove itself from the field of politics only to absorb politics into its structure, it somehow managed to maintain some semblance of vitality and forward-movement despite its structural immobility. By truncating and absorbing political discourse, neoliberalism deprived politics of the energy and belief it needed to remain operative. By transforming politics in this way – and denigrating the past and its role in creating the present – neoliberal universalism committed the terrible crime of stripping the people of a conceivable future.

Throughout the 80s and 90s, sociologists began to address the forms of social change that appeared to have paradoxically embedded themselves as fundamental features of the new era. Bauman suggested modern social structures had liquified.[12] Globalisation, ubiquitous consumerism and new technological advances had transformed human relationships, institutions, identities and biographical expectations. Ulrich Beck and Tony Giddens used a different range of phrases, concepts and rhetorical devices to describe a similar range of processes and effects.[13,14]

The obtuse meanderings of the postmodernists appeared to have been interpreted, understood and quietly put into action. Western society really did appear to be abandoning the structures of the past. It was not that these structures and institutions were abandoned as postmodern society sought to constitute itself anew as a *tabula rasa*. Rather, structures and institutions retained their basic functions but were stripped of their traditional symbolic power. They could no longer inspire the faith they needed to fulfil their core functions. Despite periodic updates, many seemed rather eerie spaces.[15] While some awkwardly tried to remain relevant, their time had passed, and the people continued to live among the ruins.

Throughout the modern age, people seemed to tread predictable biographical paths.[16] Now there seemed to be abundant opportunities to choose. Growing numbers of young people were free to go to university. They were free to identify their preferred career rather than being shunted unceremoniously towards the main regional employers. They were free to marry, postpone marrying or disavow entirely the institution of marriage. They were increasingly free to move between one relationship and another free from cultural condemnation. They were free to rent or buy a house and free to move to another part of the country to pursue their passions. And they could of course move to another country, take on another religion or abandon religion all together. They were free to define themselves in relation to their consumer choices rather than having an identity foisted upon them by their place of birth, the religious affiliations of their forefathers or the relative economic impediments faced by their parents or grandparents. Above all, the individual must be adaptable, flexible and ready to leave behind plans, commitments and relationships as he sought to move with the times and in pursuit of his vaguely understood market-informed 'best interests'.

Sociologists were often keen to impress upon their audience that these freedoms came at a price. The people faced an expanding range of choices, but they must also take responsibility for the choices they made. People, generally, did not glory in their new freedoms. There was no obvious upswing in human happiness, and few clear signs that the new range of choices led to fundamentally better outcomes. Choice often seemed to change little. A litany of choices frequently led to entirely predictable destinations. Poverty continued to beget poverty, and wealth continued to beget wealth.[17] Furthermore, the rapid decomposition of modernity's structures made it difficult for individuals to make informed choices about who they were, where they were going and those things to which they would give precedence in their lives. People were unsure where their choices might lead and unsure whether their favoured options would be truly satisfying. Bedevilled by unintended consequences, lives seemed more chaotic. While many people seemed to have more choices, they believed more than ever that their lives were being pushed and pulled in unpredictable directions by unknown forces. Their new freedoms seemed to induce a sense of insecurity and alienation.[18]

If this was freedom, it tended to be greeted with ambivalence.[19] Perhaps the heart wanted what it could no longer have. Perhaps the supposed freedoms of postmodern neoliberalism were not the kinds of freedoms the people truly wanted. In any case, the absence of modernity's rather rigid but functional support systems seemed to induce increasingly potent forms of anxiety.[20]

The choices we associated with the postmodern age were not all they seemed. Very often, choices were illusory or insubstantial. Many of these choices fell on the growing field of consumer practice. As Horkheimer and Adorno had long ago noted, consumer choices should not be considered an expression of freedom. The diner must choose from the menu. We could choose between a dizzying array of consumer items, but we could choose only those things made available in the marketplace.

There also remained a range of hidden inducements and expectations that seemed to strip these choices of any residual freedom. As Žižek has often stressed, offers are often made in the expectation that they will be turned down. Beneath the surface of verbal communication lies a range of protocols that tend to restrict the active choices we make about our conduct. And many of these new consumer choices seemed rather manipulative, given that, no matter what we chose, the outcome was already determined. We could choose between Sky News, BBC News, GB News and CNN, but apart from a few surface differences, the product remained the same. Thousands of kettles were available in the marketplace, but ultimately all were purchased to carry out the rudimentary task of boiling water. We could choose to work at McDonald's or Burger King or B&Q or Asda, but we would ultimately fail to secure a surplus wage and find ourselves struggling to meet the requirements for inclusion in the social and cultural mainstream.

Prospective students were given a dazzling array of data about universities, ostensibly in order to help those students make informed choices about their preferred universities.[21] Many prospective students understandably found the whirl-wind of decontextualised data mildly reassuring but ultimately unhelpful. At the end of the day, the new data didn't assist students in the task of identifying clearly which university was best for them. Most students continued to be guided by a mixture of traditional conceptions of institutional prestige and good old-fashioned gut-feeling.

Expansive consumer choices existed, but they were often rather shallow and yielded little of the gratification they seemed to promise. While consumer choices seemed to expand, fundamental features of social and economic life were not opened up to the choices of ordinary people. The people were not able to choose a political party that would blow away the cloud of permanent austerity. They could not choose full employment, low inflation and rising incomes. They could not choose economic stability and material prosperity. They could not choose to be friendly or hostile to other nations. Nor could they choose to disempower the financial elites who had clearly become the principal beneficiaries of the neoliberal economic model.

What the people got was the appearance of choice and suggestions of increased self-determination. But these falla-cious prizes were scoped up in an environment increasingly devoid of the structures that could give value, stability and meaning to ordinary lives. Collective identities were beginning to break apart. The solace of religion was increasingly inac-cessible to a population encouraged to believe in its own disbelief. The concept of community was stripped of its sub-stance. Marriage was just a piece of paper. Friendships and romantic relationships were weighed in accordance with their perceived utility.

The framework of neoliberal capitalism remained fixed firmly in place. Time moved forward but history did not. On the surface of things, the social and cultural fields seemed increasingly defined by choice and change. It seemed like our cultural lives were less fixed and dependable. But amid this swirl of ephemeral choices, and amid the cacophony of neoliberal boosterism that sought to convince the people they were the beneficiaries of constant progress, many felt stuck and incapable of reaching out to seize the freedoms of the age.[22,23]

Rather than feeling empowered to propel their lives in a direction of their choosing, people felt assailed by doubt and buffeted by unpredictable crosswinds that seemed powerful enough to drag their lives off in an undesired direction. It was now necessary to take responsibility for one's own life. More choices and more responsibilities seemed to create a new cultural landscape replete with risks.[24] Very often people felt that no matter how diligent their planning, the future remained decidedly unpredictable.[25] One could work hard to secure qualifications, become intimately acquainted with the realities of one's favoured industries, research key employers, move across the country, transform one's identity and demeanour to better fit the corporate archetype and still find oneself marooned in the downgraded labour markets one set out to avoid. One could save and save and save for the deposit for a house and then be crippled by rising interest rates or rendered destitute by a collapse in house prices. Choices may have risen, but, in a context of ongoing resource reallocation and permanent austerity, these choices were not leading the majority towards more satisfying and secure lives.

This should not be read as a critique of choice or an attempt to give precedence to some other source of value. Rather, it is a critique of the insubstantial nature of the choices postmodern neoliberalism offers. The deconstruction of the structural contexts that might enable the individual to make sound, life-enhancing choices should not be considered a portal to the realm of emancipation. Freedom without commitment is a very shallow form of freedom that deprives individuals of much that they will need to build a satisfying life. Stripping the social world of norms, values and a functional symbolic order in the hope of producing an experimental space for boundless self-creation certainly didn't lead to any noteworthy benefits for ordinary people, especially given that this new experimental space was shot through with commercial interests. The freedom to choose to whom or to what we give our commitment is a far more positive vision of freedom, but in order to make that decision, we must first possess the wherewithal to make informed choices. It is also vital that we retain the capacity to believe.

The abstracted individual who has no skin in the game does not seek the improvement of our natural, social and political environments. While we cannot be reduced to our social roles, our relationships or to the various features of our social identity, it is our attachment to these things that gives us the impetus to seek improvement. All that we have is what we know. We can use only what we know to determine what is worth knowing. Stripped of all prior existing knowledge – convinced that these forms of knowledge are holding us back and restricting our freedom – we are adrift without a reliable means of propelling ourselves forward.

5

PERMANENT REFORM

The common experience of rootlessness and disorientation also has a crucial institutional context. Many readers of this book will be keenly aware that our core institutions have changed a great deal in a relatively short period of time. As neoliberalism began to establish itself as an unchallengeable orthodoxy and as postmodernism worked its magic on the cultural stage, our core institutions embarked upon a process of continuous reform. This process subtly aimed to eliminate many of modernity's collectivist and universalist social conventions. These conventions were replaced with principles that emphasised individualism, isolationism and the separation of financial and economic matters from institutional culture and managerial practice. Where once core institutions seemed reasonably static, now they would be animated by an abiding commitment to constant motion. As neoliberalism moved with purpose into the 21st century, it strategically sought to soften its image in the hope of securing its continuity. The heartlessness of hardcore economic liberalism merged with cherry-picked elements of the left's cultural activism to establish the ideological framework of progressive neoliberalism.[1] Unsurprisingly, the Professional Managerial Class

(PMC) was handed the responsibility of leading our institutions into the new world.

The PMC is a thoroughly overhauled and ostensibly progressive elite that some believe is responsible for much of the cultural turbulence and political discord associated with the latter half of neoliberal era.[2] However, while the PMC is indeed a powerful elite worthy of critique, it is a mistake to believe that it had control of the tiller and was steering the ship as our nations entered the perpetual storm of depoliticised, technocratic neoliberalism.[3] In fact, the PMC is a sub-dominant elite: an elite that protects the interests of the true elites, who for the most part derives their power from concentrated wealth.[4] In return for high-profile roles in our core institutions, the PMC promulgates a shallow instrumental version of progressive ideology and maintains the myth that traditional sources of authority will be reformed in the interests of the people. While the populist right fulminate at the irrationality and sanctimony of this new management elite, it predictably fails to notice that it manages in the interests of a far more powerful elite determined to maintain its supremacy while denying its deleterious impact upon the social world.

As neoliberalism evolved, the PMC replaced the old conservative management class and resolutely applied itself to the task of overhauling our institutions. For the most part, this involved dispensing with the inefficiencies, blockages and exclusions associated with the old way of doing things. What appeared to be a more humanistic approach needed to be adopted. One of the first characteristics to undergo change was the old image of institutional authority. Out went the old, pinstriped, male-dominated sternness of the past. In came what seemed to be a more sensitive, inclusive and adaptable model, save for the fact that, beneath the surface, a vociferous commitment to protecting the fundaments of neoliberal economics remained very much in place.

Many institutional leaders had grasped the benefits of a liberal education and imagined their ideological commitments to be beyond logical dispute. Of particular importance was the increasingly ubiquitous belief that the past is typified by horrific bigotry and inhumanity. The PMC, who were by this stage at the head of most of our institutions and corporations, magnanimously acknowledged the involvement of these various entities in the horrors of the past and pledged to do what they could to drive reconciliation while ensuring that the horrors did not return.

They also approached the task of institutional management differently. Often, they sought to present themselves as friends and equals rather than the bearer of institutional authority. On first-name terms with their underlings, they did what they could to create the impression that they were fully invested in the work of the institution and committed to the shared tasks that patterned the working lives of its employees. Keen to acknowledge the mistakes of the past, they also wanted to be seen as dedicated to driving positive change, unearthing and discarding flawed work practices and ensuring that employees felt free to express themselves. They also began to institute a welter of meetings that served to maintain the myth of democratic oversight, and a range of new training and educational courses that served to promulgate the reformed ideology of the institution's new management class.

Rather than inundate employees with blunt demands, the new generation of managers tended to make solicitous requests for assistance. But amid the stage-managed informality echoed the traditional voice of institutional power. For example, managers may ask if, in order to overcome a particular challenge, an underling would mind working over the weekend. Would it be too much trouble? Of course, on the surface of things, the employee has a choice. The employee is not being simply told they must work over the weekend. Formally, they have the option to say no. Of course, the formal suggestion of choice is a red herring. No choice exists. The employee is expected to announce that they would be happy to work over the weekend. Taking the managers question at face value could prove calamitous.[5]

The studied faux informality of institutional managers seemed to possess a veneer of positivity and progress. Old barriers seemed to be breaking down, allowing more informal and mutually supportive work cultures to emerge. Managers could really get to know their underlings. The old hierarchies were silly and counterproductive. But, in many respects, there was a greater degree of honesty in the old system. And the new emphasis on humanistic informality did not spell the end of the perennial threat of redundancy for those who failed to adequately align themselves with the interests of the institution. As most employees of large corporations can attest, every now and then the mask of humanistic empathy and tolerance falls to reveal the unfeeling and often brutal reality that continues to reside beneath.

The new system seemed replete with choices, but the choices only served to disguise the insistent demand that all employees fall into line. Mightn't one say that the new system was more brutal than the old, given that it constantly mobilised the symbolic power of choice despite the fact that no real choice existed? Is the employee, who is told without explanation that they must work over the weekend, in some respects better off than the employee who is asked politely if he or she would mind working over the weekend, only to find themselves compelled to lie to the boss by announcing that they'd be happy to do it? As the boss leaves the office, the employee working under the old system swears at the injustice of being forced to work against her wishes. The employee working under the new system swears at himself for being so stupid as to wilfully accept work he does not want to do.

Like many core institutions, large corporations took up the challenge of constant reform. Change was necessary and inherently good. Work practices had to be subjected to constant evaluation with a view to identifying and correcting archaic practices and attitudes. Outdated practices and attitudes had to be dragged into the light where they could be dispensed with, allowing the corporation to become fitter, leaner and better prepared for the challenges that were assumed to lie ahead. Those identified as possessing views, attitudes or approaches to work not in keeping with the institution had to change or leave. Even if one's work was exemplary, one's job was in jeopardy if one's private beliefs were discovered to be in marked contrast with those of the organisation.

Employees were also required to have their skills periodically updated to ensure that the corporation remained adaptable and ready to compete. Corporations now seemed to demand more of their employees.[6] Being competent at core work tasks was no longer enough. And the standard nine-to-five working day was a relic from the past and had to go.[7] Employees had to be ready to contribute whenever they were needed. The standard division between employer and employee was an unhelpful anachronism. Rather than working to secure a wage, employees were expected to be emotionally invested in the interests of the corporation and committed to every task management regarded as necessary to secure its continual improvement.

In this way, many noteworthy corporations attempted to take advantage of the symbolic positivity of progressive activism. They spoke boldly about fighting racism, sexism and transphobia and tried as much as they could to make their workforce 'diverse'.[8] Their employees were often expected to join their employers and managers in these respective fights and, in aligning themselves with the 'values' of their employer, to see their employment as a form of activism. Boardrooms became more diverse, at least in terms of surface characteristics. Beneath the surface, ideological and cultural uniformity was an unacknowledged outcome of the drive to diversify in a corporate sector that remained ravenously hungry for ever greater profits. Many large corporations proclaimed their commitment to various progressive causes on social media and sought allyship with various branches of the activist left. However, they did not proclaim their willingness to boost the pay and conditions of their most exploited employees. Nor did they announce their willingness to end zero hours contracts, welcome trade unions, stop offshoring production, reduce the remuneration packages of senior management or begin the process of addressing the negative externalities of their voracious profit seeking.

In many workplaces, employees were also required to give more of themselves and to reveal more of their personalities and personal histories.[9] In some workplaces, they were called upon to divulge their innermost thoughts and feelings, which would then be subjected to ideological interrogation. This process was of course filtered through a progressive lens. On the surface of things, employers were enabling their employees to express themselves, to give free rein to their emotions and draw upon their hidden reserves, ostensibly with a view to bonding the workforce together more closely and enabling team members to recognise shared interests and concerns. These strategies suggested a new progressive informality that contrasted sharply with the restrictive corporate culture and stuffy hierarchies of the past. Beneath the surface, however, lay the standard corporate desire to extract as much applied energy from their employees as they were able to give.

Some progressive workplaces attempted to foreground 'fun'. Employees were required to tell jokes, sing or generally act the fool in front of their work colleagues.[10] Again, the goals of such strategies seemed positive, open and progressive. People were being invited to enjoy their work. However, organised fun is usually no fun at all. Most employees asked to engage in such practices greeted them with dread. The employer's request to act the fool was encoded and interpreted as a direct order. The employee was required to let go of her dignity and do as instructed, in what were often cringeworthy moments enjoyed only by those in positions of power and only because they were indicated the continuation of power imbalances that had supposedly been left behind. Modern work cultures displayed myriad abuses and injustices, but for the most part, the employer hoped only to exploit the labour of his employees. In many contemporary work cultures, the employer's demands spread much further, encroaching upon the privacy and emotional lives of employees with ever greater vigour.

The emphasis placed on informality reflects the deeply embedded drive to find new ways to boost productivity. It also hides a desire to extend and reinforce control over the workforce. Employees are understood to be living, breathing exemplars of their corporate employer, and must act accordingly. Many large institutions now monitor the social media use of their employees and are ready to summarily dismiss any employees who engage in social or political activities that might reflect badly upon their employer.

Employees are also required to be 'always on'. Emails must be answered in a timely fashion. Even when the employee is encouraged not to answer emails outside of standard work hours, in these increasingly competitive and anxiety-laden work cultures this apparently magnanimous suggestion is constructed as a rule that we are expected to transgress. In some sectors, it is inviting trouble not to respond immediately and run the risk of losing track of particularly important email. There is also a fetishistic aspect to it: checking emails often isn't too onerous and yet yields a small, fidgety sense of engagement. In some sectors, it becomes difficult to absent oneself entirely from the matrix of work-related matters, and we are enjoined to take a small measure of satisfaction from our anxiety-driven overwork. We may, for example, feel that, by doing the work immediately, we are stealing a march on our competitors. We may also feel that, by immediately completing work as it materialises, we are perversely saving ourselves the effort of doing it later. After all, the work will need to be done anyway when the working week begins. The diverse negativities of operating in such work cultures should be obvious. Even 'bullshit jobs' seemed to be demanding more of employees. Bureaucracy expanded, and genuine autonomy declined.[11] The bonds that connected us to the real world – to family, friends and community – were loosening, while the bonds that connected us to our employment and its mediation were being pulled ever tighter.

Employees were also required to commit to constant cycle of training. Often, this involved the accumulation of practical skills as their employer sought more efficient work systems and processes. Just as employees became conversant with a given online system or a particular way of working, they might quickly find that their employer had judged it inadequate and moved onto something else. No longer could one accumulate enough knowledge to conduct a corporate job effectively. Skills needed to be constantly updated to keep pace with ever-changing requirements of the job. Employees also had to be willing to change themselves – especially their views, politics and personalities – to fit in with the evolving demands of the corporate workplace. They had to be demonstrably committed to the corporation's values and interests. In exchange, some employees were able to secure a surplus wage, but the fidelity employers demanded of them was certainly not reciprocated.

This kind of perpetual change established itself as hegemonic institutional practice during the 1990s. Universities are perfect exemplars. The demand for constant change and improvement, with no end in sight, can be seen splashed on university websites and heard in the proclamations of university managers. Past performance must be improved upon, no matter how good that performance was. No matter how happy students are with the quality of their education, they must be made happier still. No matter how world-leading its research, the university must constantly strive for improvement. Replicating standard practices won't do. Being consistently good isn't good enough. Everything is rendered subject to constant change.

Apparently terrified by the prospect of standing still, the neoliberal university seemed increasingly like a neurotic who talks incessantly and fills her life with constant activity in order to endlessly postpone the moments of quiet contemplation she imagines might lead to an encounter with the fundamental causes of her sadness and discomfort. Now, even standard features of university life – a lecture or a seminar for example – cannot be allowed to remain in place. New technologies must be introduced, new strategies to engage students, new techniques that add a little glitz to the learning experience.

Ancient practices – like reading a book – must be updated, repackaged and very often made easier, more palatable or more entertaining. Many universities in the UK, for example, having accepted that their customers do not like to read and will avoid it as much as they can, have instituted new programmes that enable students to access easy to digest learning materials on their smart phones. Of course, such practices avoid the true issue and simply reconstitute a dislike for reading books as a dislike for text documents formatted for smart phones. Such practices are presented as an indication of the university's willingness to embrace change and to move away from the stifling orthodoxies of the past in order to satisfy their customers and give them what they need to prosper in a competitive and constantly changing labour market.

The university's commitment to perpetual change has of course transformed the work practices of academics. Academics themselves must volubly commit to the process of constant improvement. One of the outcomes of perpetual change is an increase in bureaucracy and administrative practices that have little to do with the traditional goals of the university. The constant need to monitor change, so that the university's commitment to change can be evidenced and improvement established as a constant feature of university life, has also created new strata of university employment. Rather than teaching or conducting research, these relatively new employees might be found creating tables and charts that outline a department's performance in terms of generating research income, publishing world-leading research or inspiring positive student feedback on the quality of its teaching. Similarly, a greater proportion of the academic workload is given over to practices that can be metricised and tabulated before being used by the university to evidence their commitment to constant improvement.

The commitment of corporations, universities and other assorted institutions to constant reform mirrored changes that were taking place throughout neoliberal society. Social and cultural change became constant but within an overarching framework that did not change. While changes themselves were often slight, they did not relent. And there existed few places where one could take refuge. Truth be told, the workplace changes described above were not simply about evolving work practices. While there are clear suggestions of a desire to exert control over workforces, nor can they be reduced to that singular aspiration. The cumulative effects of constant exposure to change throughout society and culture went deeper.

The individual was called upon to change.[12] Indeed, individuals were instructed to embrace constant change and push themselves to enjoy the unpredictability and ever-increasing turbulence of life. The individual was required to change her behaviour, demeanour, personality, attitudes and beliefs, and she must do so with few resting places and no identifiable final destination to move towards. The general effect was to encourage the individual to constantly monitor herself, to internalise the panoptic gaze of centralised authority and to critically appraise her own skills and performance along with her own attitudes and view-points. Had the individual adequately adapted to change? Had she completely let go of the past and embraced the evanescent requirements of the present? Were her skills sufficiently up to date? Could she truly claim to embody her employer's values? Did her viewpoints accord with those of others whose views mattered, or might they cause embarrassment, ostracism and unemployment were she to announce them in public?

For some, doubt and insecurity encouraged self-censure. The burden of self-censure should not be underestimated. The potential negative outcomes for an individual beset by doubts about who he is and what he believes – and doubtful about whether his identity and beliefs will be considered acceptable within the shards of the shattered social world to which he seeks admittance – can be overwhelming. For others, doubt and insecurity seem to have encouraged the construction and display of nuanced and instrumental status claims, as the anxious individual seeks to prove the extent to which he embodies the latest ephemeral trend in approved discourse.[13]

The positivity of ethical cultural review diminished rapidly as soon as it was adopted as a feature of management discourse.[14] The initial positivity of inclusion fell away and in its place were erected a range of simulated representations. Within the frame of contemporary corporate culture, workers inevitably engage instrumentally with these representations. In fact, they are encouraged to do precisely that. The evolution of management discourse inevitably produces new arenas in which one can seek personal advantage. Of course, in keeping with the emphasis upon constant ethical reform, the corporation actively solicits domesticated and truncated critique of its past and present. What matters for the corporation is that its financial model remains beyond critique and modification while the impression is created that it is an ethical contributor to society. The corporation's supposed commitment to cultural liberalism and its willingness to integrate a flattened and instrumentalised version of EDI into its management discourse is, of course, suggestive of its willingness to engage in progressive change. However, these suggestions of progressive change have been instituted in the hope of preventing or circumventing calls for fundamental change that would ultimately challenge the forms of exploitation inherent to contemporary neoliberal capitalism.

'Adapt or die' seemed to be the message vibrating along the thousands of tendrils that led from the generative core of neoliberal society to the perilous surface of everyday life. Adapt or die. Of course, as neoliberalism motored into a featureless future, many were unable to adapt sufficiently and were ruthlessly left behind. Many of those who contributed to this study believed that they had somehow found themselves outside of the main current of perpetual change and adaptation. Their views were outdated, their skills would soon be obsolete and they lacked the wherewithal to constantly transform themselves in ways that might enable them to remain competitive, compliant and included.

Many used the phrase 'clinging on' to describe their predicament. They saw themselves as perilously positioned and desperately fighting to remain connected to the social mainstream. Many lacked the resources to access the leisure practices they once enjoyed, and most struggled to buy the consumer objects that signalled cultural inclusion.[15] They also often seemed to think that they lacked the resources to retrain. It was too late for them. They'd missed the boat. They were left standing on the jetty as it sailed gently off towards its unknown destination. The jobs of the future, at least those which could be conceived, seemed totally beyond them. Many couldn't summon up the energy required to keep up the fight.

They were also often aware that their views were considered old fashioned and outdated. Things they once imagined eternal truths now seemed to have been thrown into question. It wasn't always the case that they believed their views were right and the constantly evolving views of liberal mainstream were wrong. Rather, the forms of knowledge they had developed throughout their lives were all they had to work with. These forms of knowledge had allowed them a means of understanding the world. To discard them at this stage seemed to make little sense. To even think about swapping one set of views for another was disorientating. Was it even possible to throw away fundamental forms of understanding and quickly adopt what seemed like an entirely new set of understandings? Wasn't it too late for them to make the change? Weren't they condemned to hold outdated views, views that ensured marginalisation, views that compelled one to keep quiet lest one be vilified or sanctioned in some way, views that could only receive an airing when the individual was sure they were in a safe space occupied by others likely to feel the same or at least a space in which others were less likely to seek censure? The only remaining strategy available to them was to cling on as tightly as possible to what they already had.

Most looked forward to retirement, but virtually all of those in full-time work very much wanted to keep their jobs. This may seem obvious, but I mention it because the general trend, especially for younger working-class workers, is to adopt the role of the vagrant, moving ceaselessly between one unsatisfying location and the next in a forlorn search for a place in which they might feel valued, comfortable and adequately remunerated for the work they do.[16,17] Yet with regard to this study, even those workers with very low-paying jobs hope to keep them. Few career aspirations remained. The unhappy expectation that, should they be forced to switch jobs, the next one would be worse had replaced the optimistic youthful expectation that moving regularly between employers would eventually result in the discovery of a gratifying – or at least tolerable – final destination. They aspired for their children, but for them, clinging on would have to do.

Some parents had clearly tried very hard to ensure their children were sufficiently motivated and credentialised to fight their way into a good position at the starting gate. Some also appeared to have stressed to their children the need to prepare themselves emotionally and behaviourally for the requirements of these new labour markets. Mostly, this centred on general encouragement and a continual invocation to think strategically about how to fashion future success. Often, these parents admitted that they could offer little practical guidance. But no matter how much they jostled to get their children into a good position, many worried about how their children would fare once the starting pistol was fired, and the race got underway.

These men and women felt removed from the mainstream and didn't want their children to succumb to the same fate.

But every now and then they seemed worried that their children were already the bearers of a malign cultural capital that would eventually bring about their inevitable failure. Despite their efforts, their children had somehow been stained by this place and its diverse effects. They would be revealed by their accents, demeanour and styles of communication, as if a tiny residue of the antiquated cultural attitudes of generations gone by could not be fully dispensed with and would be immediately identified by those capable of granting admittance to the new kingdom.

Many of those I interviewed were parents of adult offspring who in most cases had not improved upon the social position of their parents. In a small number of cases, they had attended university. Their parents were understandably proud. However, in each case, a university degree appeared not to have acted a springboard to the good life. Mostly, these credentialised young adults had moved away for work. The pride their parents felt was tempered by the pain of separation. Almost all had found a space in one of the routinised non-manual sectors of the economy. It was not unusual to encounter male parents working in traditional manual occupations bemoaning the financial problems faced by their newly credentialised children. These children, usually the first in their family to attend university, often appeared to be at least partially financially reliant upon their traditional working-class parents. Situations like this seemed to compound the common view that our society and economy were on the slippery slope to dysfunctionality. For many, the game seemed rigged. No matter how hard one worked, for many there would never be a genuine chance to 'make it'.

Most of my interviewees' adult offspring had moved into working-class occupations. Often, this move was not as seamless as one might imagine. It was usually necessary to navigate one's way through post-16 education before a job materialised, but nothing was guaranteed. A good proportion of the men seemed to have pursued careers in the manual trades and in the building industry. These jobs were often highly prized, and again their parents tended to express a degree of pride in their son's achievements. Becoming a qualified brick-layer or a welder suggested steady work at a good wage, certainly above what one could expect in the non-manual ser-vice sector, where most of my interviewees' children ended up. In a small number of cases, interviewees' adult children were struggling to fully establish a life of their own. These children tended to remain in the family home. Drugs, crime and mental health problems were also mentioned. These were of course quite difficult conversations. At least at home parents could keep an eye on their wayward children and do what they could to help them to find a better route forward.

Parents tended to be quite pleased when their children had found their way into reasonably settled positions. Unem-ployment, welfare dependency and poverty were the great fears. If one could stick it out, become conversant with new work requirements and establish oneself as a fixture in any given workplace, this was usually taken as a blessing. How-ever, this did not mean anxieties dissipated as soon as their children made it into a steady job. Many parents had grown accustomed to stretching their incomes carefully to ensure that some semblance of normality was maintained. Often, they would recount nostalgic tales of their own consumer excesses, all of which emanated from an all-too-brief time in their lives when they had fewer responsibilities and more disposable cash. Parents wanted similar experiences for their children. They didn't want their children to struggle. Those who had better-paying jobs tried to help out their children as much as they could. However, anxieties lingered about how they would cope with the turbulence all were sure lay ahead.

Jobs would be lost, and then what? Bad things would happen, and how would they cope?

Underneath some of this talk was the assumption that my interviewees were hardened to the ways of the world, whereas their children were not. No matter what the world threw at them, they could take it. Their children, however, hadn't struggled in the way they had. They had known poverty and experienced life's various pitfalls and challenges, whereas their children hadn't. We might reasonably assume that such sentiments reveal the common desire to imagine one's children unsullied by life's adversities. It is very common to assume that older generations had it tougher, and younger generations have been cosseted to a greater extent. It is certainly true that many of my interviewees had experienced a greater degree of poverty. The men had grown up in a tough culture that stressed autonomy, physicality and the importance of retaining dignity and respect in the face of inevitable challenges. The women too had struggled as they had sought to assert their independence, juggling the competing requirements of the old gender order with those of an increasingly competitive market society. They had grown up relatively poor, but largely unaware of their relative poverty. They had then secured jobs and established fledgling consumer identities. They married and had children. Often, they had bought a house or moved into accommodation they judged positively in relation to the house where they grew up. Some divorced. Careers lost momentum. Pay levels stagnated or fell. In most cases, it seemed unlikely that their children had experienced similar levels of poverty. Most appear to have grown up in better quality houses, with more holidays, better quality clothes and a greater variety of consumer gadgets.

Outside the family home, of course, little could be guaranteed. The schools they attended had an obviously different character, but it was debateable whether or not they were of a significantly better quality. And many dangers continued to exist in these neighbourhoods. Were these working-class kids really less equipped to deal with life's difficulties? It was difficult to tell, especially given that I only had the parents' testimony to go on. Of far more importance, within the context of this study, was the parents' perception of their children's weakness and unpreparedness. This belief may have had a foundation in reality, but it also seemed to be bound up with a broad range of multifaceted anxieties about the future. They worried about their children's weakness because they assumed they would encounter challenges with the capacity to overwhelm them. But how could their children really be better prepared for as yet unspecified negative events? Clearly, committing a perpetual cycle of retraining and accreditation was regarded as part of the solution, but there also appeared to be a general desire for their children to be more emotionally and mentally resilient. But, again, there was an obvious lack of clarity. How much emotional resilience would be enough? How much more emotionally resilient could one be without sacrificing other aspects of one's character and identity? Listening to these men and women talk, there didn't seem to be an identifiable end point. A comforting degree of security seemed unachievable. Overcoming anxieties about one facet of life would see new anxieties burst forth in another. The old securities had disappeared, and anxieties, fear and confusion seemed to be reasserting themselves as a default position.

The phrase deadaptation has been used to capture the failure of particular groups and cultures to respond produc-tively to the apparent necessity of change.[18] Not maladapta-tion, which suggests the failure to adapt adequately, but deaptation, an active movement against adaptation itself. We might reasonably suggest that the old working class has for some time found itself in a deaptative state. Rather than existing on the margins and fighting hard to move closer to the centre, these men and women often imagine themselves external to the cultural mainstream and unlikely to be granted readmittance. The world appeared to be changing in unpredictable ways, and they couldn't keep up. Indeed, many suggested they didn't want to keep up even though they suspected it was in their interests to do so. The way the world was changing often didn't appear to make much sense.

It is of course possible to categorise this response as a reaction formation.[19] Do these men and women actually want to adapt in the hope of being accepted into the mainstream but adopt the opposite position because they are anxious that any such efforts will inevitably be rebuffed? It is not clear. Occasionally, those who discussed these issues seemed to oscillate between the two positions, expressing a desire to move on and succeed in one moment, only to assume adaptation was impossible in the next. There were many discussions in which interviewees mocked the mainstream for its perceived illogicality and general weirdness. However, very often these discussions also involved an acknowledgement that the mainstream seemed illogical from *their subjective position*. While there were jokes about cultural fads and so on, these were almost always accompanied by self-deprecating talk about getting old, being 'out of the loop', and so on. Rather than simply claiming that the mainstream was illogical, they tended to claim that it was illogical *to them*.

While many accepted that they would be unable to change themselves in ways that might allow re-entry to the mainstream, they were still very often ambitious for their children. They wanted their sons and daughters to remain viable as adaptable employees even if that meant moving away from home, changing their persona and setting aside the cultural characteristics they had absorbed during their youth. These discussions were often laden with emotion. Many, in their heart of hearts, wanted their lives to remain intertwined with those of their children and grandchildren. They wanted their children to enjoy the earthy delights of the vibrant culture they had known. But they also accepted that to stay was to fail. Success was out there somewhere but certainly not here. Their children needed to unsentimentally commit to their future material success.

As we have already seen, the brutal economic logic that underpins the abandonment of the old working class is softened by an accompanying cultural critique that vilifies that class as inherently regressive and incompatible with the ideological requirements of future-facing liberal society. External to a reformed, simulated and consumerised mainstream, they thoughtlessly reproduce the cultures and ideologies that led to their exclusion in the first place. Left to the care of their incorrigible parents, children thoughtlessly take on characteristics, attitudes, viewpoints and identities that will actively prevent them from accessing the alluring rewards that seem to be immediately available in the cultural mainstream. Those children who have the wherewithal to fight their way free from their own personal histories, succeed in the post-sixteen education system and accumulate the cultural characteristics of the progressive mainstream have an outside chance of finding a place at the centre. But it is only an outside chance.

It is not that capitalism no longer needs working-class labour. Rather it is that capitalism is fully aware that a fractured working class has nowhere else to go. It has been defeated as a political force and sucked dry as a source of cultural creativity. It has lost the institutions that once signalled unity and common purpose. It is hopelessly fragmented and no longer has the wherewithal to push back against aggressive exploitation. Forced into what seems like an irreversible retreat, its wages have stagnated, its buying power has fallen, its status has declined and many of the state services that, during the modern era, gave it a chance to progress have fallen into disrepair or disappeared entirely. Contemporary capitalism may still need working-class labour, but it no longer needs to apply effort to sustain the relationship.[20]

Modern western industrialism is dead. The British working class has not been needed as a productive industrial workforce for decades. However, there remains a huge amount of work to be done keeping civil society and its diverse consumer markets afloat. Working-class labour remains vital to the smooth functioning of most sectors of the practical economy. However, the key point is that the forms of labour that tend to fall to the working class no longer signal inclusion in contemporary capitalism's simulated social world. This might strike us as strange, given that it still makes sense to suggest that the working class constitute the majority of the population.[21] However, while the modern political fight was to advance the interests of the entire working class, very often today the central fight for young working-class men and women is to leave the working class behind as they attempt to make the journey towards a vague new world that seems better.

Bereft of cultural confidence, organisation and institutional support, the contemporary working class can be ruthlessly disregarded and exploited to a much greater degree. In the face of neoliberalism's onslaught, the impetus for many is to fight their way to something that looks like safe ground. However, many can't get out of the way of this onslaught. Some can't conceive of being anything other than what they are already. Others are forced to remain so tightly focused on their immediate material welfare that they can't begin to strategically move out of the line of fire. And others, of course, cannot develop the resources that will appeal to the corporate employers of the future. They're running in the right direction, fighting with all their might to make it to safety, but seem destinated to fall short.

Whatever remained of the working-class's defensive lines have crumbled. Atomised workers are now in a full disorderly retreat. Unable to unify, politicise, accept the reality of their predicament and finally turn to face their adversary, an unseemly scramble has ensued. Members of the contemporary working class are forced to compete against one another for the scraps that fall from the oligarchs table or for the down-graded forms of work needed to keep neoliberalism's simulated social world in some kind of order.

For many, buying a home has become an impossible dream. Renting a property with the space for a family is often immensely difficult. Much working-class work is poorly paid, unreliable and devoid of positive symbolism. Some interviewees were in receipt of housing benefit, which of course reflects the inadequacy of their wages and the broader injustices of their employment. Poor wages have a multitude of negative knock-on effects. Often, individuals and families are forced to focus on navigating immediate problems, which makes planning strategically for future success challenging to say the least.[22] But the growing instability of life in these places has many diverse features.

Decades of incessant and often high-paced change have stripped many working-class neighbourhoods of the commonality that once acted as a platform for modern socialism. Some of the men and women I spoke to noted that they often feel strangely set apart from the places they call home. These places no longer feel like themselves, as if they had somehow lost their fundamental essence. The environments themselves looked much the same but no longer conveyed to them a deep sense of familiarity and relative comfort. The neighbourhoods they knew best seemed somehow out of sync with the powerful situated memories and affective ties that once allowed the individual to construct and maintain a meaningful sense of home. In a strange twist, their memories of the past seemed stable and honest despite the fact that memories inevitably fade and warp with the passage of time. In comparison, the reality of their neighbourhoods in the here and now – a world they could see, hear and touch – seemed somehow inauthentic, absent of some hidden substance once present but now lost.

The relationship these people had to their neighbourhoods seemed to have broken down. Often, while discussing these matters, it wasn't clear if the breakdown was irreparable or if the outward expression of such sentiments was largely a symptom of other forms of change destabilising the lives of those I spoke to. Mood was important. Perceptions of the places could change slightly, depending on the nature of our conversation. However, such observations were clearly significant and worthy of further investigation. While much talk about the neighbourhood's past was positive and stirred nostalgic memories, talk of its present circumstances tended to communicate a general sense of negativity and disappointment. It is, of course, difficult to discuss a growing sense of estrangement from one's home environment. These are weighty matters, and it is often difficult to find the words to express the range of feelings and attitudes that seemed to foment the belief that this once vital relationship was either changing or breaking apart entirely.

There were of course obvious changes to the materiality of these neighbourhoods. Some symbolically important buildings had been demolished and replaced. Others had been left to fall into rack and ruin. In some places, the layout of roads had changed, giving neighbourhoods a marginally different feel. Pubs had shut. Shops had shut. But these were only surface changes. Putting one's finger on what precisely had changed to evoke this feeling of estrangement was frustratingly difficult and, in our discussions, people tended to fall back on phrases like 'something's missing' or 'it's just not the same somehow'.

Many did, however, talk of friends and family moving away. Those who had been familiar had been replaced by those who were unfamiliar. Old characters synonymous with the neighbourhood and its history had died. Old friends and acquaintances had moved to new housing developments on the edge of town. Others had moved much further afield, usually for work. Those who moved out tended not to return. It was difficult for my interviewees to say with any certainty who had moved into the neighbourhood and from whence they came, and that seemed to be precisely the issue. They remained strangers.

In time, of course, relationships develop. Awkwardness breaks down as strangers begin to communicate, common interests and concerns are identified, and slowly new affective ties can be forged. There were a few tentative signs of this taking place, but it would be untrue to suggest that a new community was beginning to emerge amongst the ruins of the old. Overall, those I spoke to tended to accept growing diversity as an inevitability, but they were far more welcoming to those who seemed keen to integrate into the cultural life of the neighbourhood. It really helped if new arrivals were chatty and ready with a joke and a smile.

Overall, it wasn't ethnic and religious diversity that fundamentally challenged community continuity. At least not in a direct and unmediated way. Of far more importance was the churn factor.[23] People would move in and then move out before relationships could be formed. Increasingly it seemed that everyone wanted to be somewhere else. Coming and going was an established neighbourhood norm. There also seemed to have been an associated move from the public to the private realm. People kept to themselves to a much greater extent. There were fewer opportunities to stop and talk to one's neighbours. The cumulative effect of these changes seemed to inform feelings of community decomposition and estrangement. What was once familiar seemed increasingly unfamiliar. On the surface, the neighbourhood was pretty much the same, but for these men and women it *felt* different. It stirred in them different emotions and sentiments, most of which seemed to be tied to loss in some way.

6

INTIMATIONS OF POST-SOCIALITY

The working class increasingly occupy a separate stratum, as set apart from the economic mainstream as they are from the cultural mainstream. Their work helps to maintain the mainstream, but it does not guarantee their inclusion within it. As I have stressed elsewhere, the standard sociological focus on the dynamics of inclusion and exclusion is rather limited.[1] It is not simply that some are granted access to the joys of contemporary sociality while others are not. Rather, the social – properly understood – has been excluded from multiple dimensions of our lives. The public realm has been privatised, consumerised and stripped of many of its positive features. We tend not to understand our own identities and interests as being bound up with those of others. And our interests increasingly lean towards the private rather than the public realm. Affective ties are simulated and replicated, and every now and then we can catch sight of the instrumentality that seems to underpin simulated sociability.

It was common for my interviewees to acknowledge that they are, in their everyday lives, concerned principally with their own troubles, focused on the welfare of their own

families and absorbed in the allure of small consumer pleasures and multiple mass mediated distractions. They were
increasingly disengaged from the world outside. They passed
through the public realm to do what they needed to do, before
returning to the comforts of the private realm. Of course, in
adopting such routines, they tended to conduct themselves in
similar ways to those they criticised for being insufficiently
community-minded. They tended to understand their own
privatism as an effect rather than a cause. Against their
wishes, they found themselves backing slowly away from a
public realm denuded of the positive features of modern
community life.

It is the perception of absence that is again key here. These
people believed something was missing. Something once present had been withdrawn. This perceived absence encouraged
them to retreat to the private realm, which inevitably rein-
forced the processes they believed spurred their own grudging
privatism. Ultimately, the outcome was the same: a post-social
world absent of unscripted intersubjective encounters, meaningful neighbourliness, the earthy pleasures of community life
and an abiding sense that one is precisely where one is supposed to be. It is also worth briefly noting that many spoke of
enjoying their involvement in this research project because it
forced them to leave work and home behind and venture out
into the public realm. They disconnected from the hubbub of
their daily routines. They disconnected from screens and were
encouraged to speak about topics that so often remain
unspoken. It was in the public realm – walking around their
old neighbourhoods, looking at past workplaces, schools and
so on – that their nostalgia became most acute and commu-
nicable. Paul commented thus:

'It's nice, isn't it, just to talk. You get into a routine.
You end up talking about the same kinds of things to the
same people, over and over. It's nice to think about things.

I don't think I do that enough. We're all so busy nowadays, tear-arsing around from one thing to another. You don't get the time to think. These walks have got me thinking more. Stuff I'd forgotten. Probably some stuff I've avoided thinking about. It's a skill, isn't it, another skill we've lost. I'm so tired now, I get home from work and that's it, you just zone out. Now, Jesus, I've got to think about when I was a kid, parents, growing up, stuff I haven't thought about for years. You're so focused on now you forget about then. It's hard to even imagine there was a then, do you know what I mean? It seems so far away. I've had to work hard thinking'.

Dougie made a similar point:

'It's hard work, isn't it, this remembering. Walking around, everything seems so different to how I remember it. And I really haven't given it much thought til now. I've been thinking more and more about when I was young. I've been thinking about what's happened [to places like this]. It still seems all fucked to me. Something's missing I can't put my finger on. But I've been thinking on it. It's probably doing me good but it's hard work'.

In *Aesthetics of Disappearance*, Virilio focuses on decomposition and change and in particular on the role of technology in the disappearance of traditional forms of representation and experience.[2] The rapid quickening of the pace of everyday life has, for Virilio, rendered traditional forms of perception obsolete. But this is not a positive vision of a people no longer fettered to the regressive rules of the past, at long last free to reconstruct themselves in relation to their desires. Virilio is concerned principally with loss. Our grip on reality has weakened. Sources of value and traditional ways of knowing have disappeared, as have tried and tested strategies that might once have enabled us to productively tackle our most pressing problems. Hypermobility and the speed of information exchange have compressed time and space, blurring distinctions between the real and the virtual, the present and the past. As these distinctions have blurred, we have lost our ability to use our experiences to position ourselves in the world. Our sense of self has become strangely decentred and absent of the clarity that once fixed the modern individual to particular places, processes and people. We have lost our appreciation of the vastness of history and our ability to discern and appreciate the historical processes that have shaped our experiences of the present. And as history has been truncated and commodified, we have lost our ability to learn from it. Without the ability to narrativise history and position ourselves within its deep processes, we become disoriented, trapped in a perpetual present, unable to produce realistic representations of the future that speak knowledgeably to where we have been and where we are now.

Listening to participants talk vaguely about their alienation from their own neighbourhoods also brought to mind Baudrillard's multifaceted critique of postmodern consumer societies.[3] In some respects, they seem to be suggesting that they encountered the present reality of their neighbourhoods as a mere simulation, a strangely unsatisfying copy of a lost world of authenticity and wholeness. The neighbourhood looked the same, and while they couldn't put their finger on precisely what had changed, it seemed to them mysteriously absent of the *je ne sais quoi* of authentic community life. They claimed that an authentic world had existed in the past, and they could recount detailed stories they believed might evidence their claims. But also imminent in those interviews was a sense that their understanding of the world and their place within it had been destabilised by the pace of change. They seemed to feel unable to come to terms with the present and step confidently into the future. Indeed, this was one of the clearest and most compelling findings across the entire dataset. The forms of understanding they had developed earlier in life seemed redundant, as if they were stuck using ill-suited tools to address difficult and constantly evolving problems. Just as they complained at the pace of technological change – checking out their own shopping, trying to navigate a banking system suddenly absent of employees and adapt to a world increasingly mediated by apps and new technological inter-faces, etc. – they also complained about the pace of a broad array of social, cultural and economic changes. Everything seemed to be changing rapidly, even when changes did not appear to result in improvement.

They did not complain bitterly about change. Rather, the fundamental effect of multifaceted change seemed to be the disorientation identified by Virilio as a fundamental charac-teristic of the present. They couldn't keep up. They felt old before their time. They hankered after a world that made immediate sense to them, a world where they didn't have to constantly think about what was required of them, a world governed by the forms of logic and understanding that had been imprinted upon them during their youth. They seemed to be flailing around, trying to find a foothold that would allow them to steady themselves before making another attempt to come to terms with the world as it is. However, in their more ruminative moments, all seemed to agree that something vital – and perhaps timeless – had been lost, and nothing compa-rable had emerged to replace it.

In tandem with a perceived decline in authenticity and symbolic efficiency, we have also seen a precipitous decline in the positive symbolism associated with working-class labour.[4] Working-class work is simply not valued in the way that it once was, and of course, many workers are keenly aware of this fact. Some continued to enjoy some aspects of their work, but many others saw little that was appealing in their day-to-day labours. This was especially true of those who worked in the downgraded service sector.[5] And some, of course, were able to cast their minds back to times when things were very different.

It is increasingly common for those ensconced in the social and cultural mainstream to see the working class as simply there to do the jobs that no one else wants to do, providing the services that keep the lives of the professional middle class ticking over, cleaning offices, servicing cars, fixing boilers, getting rid of trash and keeping those believed to possess more valuable skills sufficiently caffeinated.[6] For many who have achieved a measure of success, the assumption is that we live in a meritocracy in which educational achievement is valued and rewarded. Hard work pays off.[7] Those who fail to move up are assumed to be lazy or insufficiently skilled. Of course, this worldview bolsters the belief that their own relative success is fully justified. Rare skills justify higher wages. Those without sufficient skills should retrain or accept their position at the bottom of the labour market.

Such views accord neatly with the progressive aspects of contemporary middle-class political culture.[8] Middle-class voters can, for example, argue in favour of an open border policy that will bring in workers willing to carry out poorly paid jobs unwanted by Britain's own working-class citizenry. On the surface, such an argument displays the usual features of progressive liberalism. Many on the activist left now call for open borders.[9] However, beneath the surface lies the unseemly assumption that we can import a low-wage workforce of immigrants who should be grateful for the opportunity to move into the most exploitative and demeaning forms of work presently available.[10] As is so often the case, progressive liberal politics resolutely refuse to address the economic realities that shape labour markets and most aspects of our culture. They do not argue that wages should rise, that exploitation should be brought to an end, that businesses reliant upon incredibly low wage levels contribute nothing of value, or that every worker should be able to earn a wage that guarantees a genuine stake in civil society. Instead, we overlook the brutal reality of exploitation by daubing it in the vibrant colours of progressive liberalism. This approach also contains an unfair criticism of Britain's poorest. Why do they not accept these low-paying jobs? Are they lazy, indulged by the great bounty dispensed by the stripped-back welfare state, or perhaps they feel unjustifiably entitled to well-paying jobs they are not qualified to carry out, and are content to remain at their leisure until one turns up? Of course, here we encounter a clear indication of the close relationship between cultural liberalism and economic liberalism, between the progressive left and the neoliberal right, a relationship integral to the ruling ideology at the end of history. Left liberalism and right liberalism are presented as opposites, but they are anything but.

Of much greater importance is the implicit assumption that low-wage work is a timeless feature of our economy. Rather than arguing about who will carry out the most poorly paid jobs, the truly progressive approach is to demand that low-paying jobs are immediately dispensed with. Jobs that do not pay employees enough to live a reasonably satisfying life do not make a positive contribution to our nation and its citizens. Businesses that rely on incredibly low wage levels should not be considered viable businesses. In most cases, incredibly low rates of pay are used to secure high profits and high salaries for senior managers. To maximise profit, it is necessary to reduce costs to an absolute minimum. The ostensibly progressive drive to continually import workers willing to accept poverty wages is a form of progressivism tied to the ongoing interests of neoliberalism and the obscene forms of economic injustice upon which it depends.

Working-class labour was at the very centre of the modern industrial age.[11] Working-class trade unions were once able to shape industrial policy and influence governmental decision-making.[12] Many members of the working class believed that, in their day-to-day labours, they were contributing to the well-being of the nation. Their skills were valued. As a class, they had moved away from the terrible poverty of the pre-war age. They remained at the bottom of the social and economic hierarchy, but the incline was gentler and its upper reaches less distant. And perhaps more importantly, it was not compulsory to attempt to fight one's way up the hill. It was possible to live a full and satisfying life within the working class, enjoying local cultures and pastimes and building and sustaining nourishing relationships with others. Poverty continued to exist, and there existed a multitude of problems and injustices that clearly run contrary to suggestions that this was a golden age, but much that was good about the modern age has clearly disappeared, and much that we are told is positive about contemporary western societies has simply failed to bear fruit for ordinary people.[13]

Many interviewees expressed sentiments in keeping with the model of deaptation I briefly outlined above. Beyond their extended social circle and the environments that represented home, many couldn't see where they fitted in. They felt set apart from politics and external to popular culture. Many continued to be dedicated but resource poor consumers, but what was this world they saw on their TVs? What were they supposed to make of the world as it was presented on the BBC? Many felt out of the loop, condemned by the attitudes and expectations that had been impressed upon them during their youth. As the world seemed to hurtle into the future, they sat marooned in their dead environments, cogitating on precisely why the truths of the past no longer seemed to hold.

Heidegger uses the phrases *throwness* to describe our experience of inhabiting a world neither of our choosing nor of our creation.[14] We cannot alter the fact of our birth, and we cannot change the historical and cultural contexts that inevitably shape our lives. It is not for us to choose the familial circumstances into which we are born and nor can be pick which socio-economic class we will inhabit. We do not strategically choose the historical moment into which we are born. These contexts exist beyond our control, and we must navigate our way through them as best we can. All we have as we attempt to interpret the world around us is our past experience. Our understanding of being, which Heidegger attempts to capture with his concept of Dasein, is irrevocably tied to the past and the tools it has bequeathed to us as we attempt to live authentically in the present. To live authentically, according to Heidegger, we must acknowledge our own thrownness, recognise the forces that shape our existence, take responsibility for our choices and face up to the finality of death.

My interviewees have not chosen the features of the world they presently inhabit and nor do they feel themselves responsible for their creation. Rather, they feel as if an incrementally more ungratifying world has been imposed upon them by external forces they cannot accurately identify. Their experience of this world is inevitably shaped by their personal histories. They know that it was once possible to feel more secure, ensconced in an environment shaped by comprehensible, shared meanings, surrounded by people comfortable in their own skin and happy to fashion a life amid a reasonably organic common culture. Memories of this lost and often idealised world inevitably shape their evaluation of the present.[15] It is not just that they evaluate the present negatively because it is absent of the positive features they believed existed in the past. Rather, it is that this positive past is all they have to measure the present against. They cannot compare their present to other presents elsewhere in the world, and nor can they compare their present to an unknowable future which, as they journey away from their situational and temporal ideal, seems to be increasingly distant and forbidding.

Often, nostalgics are denounced for their desire to go back, as if they wanted to reverse the flow of chronological time and recreate a world that aligns with their values, ideals and desires. However, with regard to those who participated in this study, this was not the case at all. What they want, in their heart of hearts, was rather the opposite. They want to transport the positive features they believe existed in the past into the present and potentially continue them into the future. And perhaps more to the point, they wanted these positive features to enrich the lives of all. They were not myopically concerned with their own narrow interests. Positive things had existed in the past but were absent from the present. They wanted these positive things to be reintroduced and developed. They wanted everyone to be able to benefit from the clarity of meaning and the forms of support and security that were once a fundamental feature of everyday life.

And what of this dire future participants seemed sure would soon materialise? It will be a product of what already exists; a creation of deep structures and processes developed in the past and adapted in the present, a collection of rolling processes of change influenced by contest and argument, the management and manipulation of belief and disbelief and underpinned by concentrated power and the evolution of the material world. And just as my interviewees used their past experiences and prior knowledge to interpret a rapidly changing world that did not accord with their preferences, so it will be for generations that follow. But that is by no means all there is to say about this current era of negativistic change. Our present era is a time of continuity and fracture, a time of rapid, depoliticised change over which we seem to have no control, a time when it has become impossible to deny that the Enlightenment principle of ongoing incremental social progress is at an end and that the future is likely to be significantly worse.

As we have seen, the children of my research participants are often judged to have missed out on something vital that would've elevated their social experience. They are private, adaptable and mobile but also apparently less secure, less grounded and unable to call upon committed assistance and support. As they head into the future, they will use the forms of knowledge established in the present to make sense of this new world. Can we say that they will be nostalgic for the denuded post-social world of the here and now? Will they see today's present as comprehensible, secure and positive when it is transformed into the future's past? Will they accept the flux of the present as an unavoidable feature of our world and learn to live with, and perhaps enjoy, this flux? To what extent will the reality of the present be idealised in memory, and how will those idealised memories be categorised and used by those in the future? It is difficult to tell. However, it seems again vital to note that it is not simply change itself that prompts the widespread sense of disorientation. Rather it is the pace of change that makes the world increasingly alien to those without the desire or the capacity to keep up. Social evolution – shaped by identifiable processes and adaptive logic – has been replaced by constant commodified and depoliticised social and cultural revolution, a drive to disturb all that seemed settled and to dispense with all that was once believed to be known. And it is at this point that we must return to politics. How can we respond politically to the travails of the present, and how can the field of politics again exhort some influence over the direction we take into the future? Must we somehow come to accept that our present trajectory will carry us inevitably to continued decline?

7

TOWARDS A BETTER FUTURE

It is usually considered compulsory to close a book of this kind with a note of optimism and positivity. Unfortunately, I cannot bring myself to do that. The gathering consensus seems to be that the road ahead takes us deeper into something resembling a new feudal era.[1] The super-rich will separate themselves entirely from the social body and use their huge wealth to steer politics, culture and our economies in ways that favour their interests. Our economies will become increasingly monopolistic and oligopolistic, manipulated by algorithms and technological surveillance and managed by new AI systems. The working class will morph into a servant class reliant upon either the crumbs that fall from the super-elite's table or upon unstable and poorly remunerated gig work providing services to the trimmed down urban professional classes who administer our institutions in the interests of elite. As we have seen, democracy is already a shadow of its former self, an increasingly hollow ritual that changes nothing.

For the moment, it is impossible to identify a sufficiently powerful countervailing force that might prevent our continued descent. The rise of post-crash populism has enlivened political debate somewhat, but it has yet to truly disrupt the prevailing dogma of neoliberal economics. Even the far right today seem deeply committed to the myths of liberal, classical and neoclassical economics and ignorant of the latent power of the currency-issuing state. The clash of ideologies, if such a phrase is appropriate in times of banal consensus, is staged entirely on the field of culture. The field of political economy continues to remain very much off limits.

I can hold out a few slivers of hope. It is still possible for the political left to rehabilitate itself and once again set itself to the task of improving the lives of ordinary people. It is possible for the radical and intellectual elements of the left to withdraw from the interminable hostility and entrenched animus of contemporary cultural politics and seek to unify various cultural groups in a grand project concerned principally with providing ordinary people with sustainable, meaningful, well-paid and secure jobs and the various services ordinary people need to build satisfying lives. It is also possible that the mainstream left will at some point in the future feel compelled to distance itself from the continued failure of neoliberalism and tentatively return to standard features of left-of-centre economic management. It is possible but, for the time being, highly unlikely. The moment for such things seems to have passed. It is also possible that a new left populism may arise and stake out a clear, logical and informed position on the field of political economy, draw disparate communities together and set to work building a better future for all. Unfortunately, there are no signs of such a movement anywhere on the horizon.

It seems more likely that change in the west will result from an intervention by an external force rather than from the internal dynamics of our political systems. The rise of the BRICS continues to threaten America's global dominance, and there has already been a partial withdrawal from the once-unchallengeable doctrine of global 'free trade'.[2] But again, it would be a mistake to immediately place our faith in the BRICS and their ability to disrupt the west's political and economic status quo. Even if they continue to draw more nations into their orbit – and even if their networks and agreements generally empower sovereign nation states, and the group remain committed to peace, national security, multipolarity and development – there are no guarantees. Nor can we say for sure that the incremental advance of the BRICS will not be met by a military response from the established western powers. It is already possible to detect our information systems attempting to orchestrate the popular mood and subtly prepare the ground for the wars of the future.

If we really want the west to change – if we really want to ensure that every citizen has what they need to live a secure and meaningful life – it behoves the politically aware in the west to engage in the kinds of transformative politics that can puncture the thin veneer of neoliberal conventions and impose a new vision of democracy, economic justice and social order upon our vacuous institutions and ossified social and political systems. If we cannot put aside cultural enmity and accept that others who possess marginally different cultural values and outlooks may actually be steadfast political allies in the fight to create a better world, then we will remain in the mire, spinning our wheels, unable to move forward, subject to a rolling project of diminishment and decrepitude as the investment class continue to pick hungrily at the bones of a once thriving civil society.

Many noteworthy authors have claimed that a crisis or an event of great magnitude may jolt us out of our inertia and return us to history.[3] Historic events of this kind open up a space of genuine contestation in which the route ahead has yet to be determined. It is here that a new politics can grow, attract commitment and move off to shape the future.

However, transformative events of this kind can only be fully understood in retrospect. Potentially transformative events pass us by all of the time and can often be manipulated and used to reassert the dominance of ruling ideas. The global financial crisis of 2008 was clearly an event of huge importance. It revealed a range of fundamental problems associated with regulating the financial economy, the anti-social opportunism that animates abstract investment markets and the continued importance of the state in supervising and directing the nation's economic affairs. Rather than being orientated to equilibrium, the abstract investment markets that had become hegemonic within post-modern neoliberal economies were deeply flawed and woefully regulated, and it fell to the supposedly moribund nation state to clean up the mess.

The evangelism that accompanied early neoliberalism quietened down somewhat, but, in the absence of a countervailing politics, neoliberalism simply continued by default. Nothing existed from which we might have fashioned a new economic model. No genuine alternatives were presented to the people. This was really the start of the technocratic age of neoliberalism. No longer did anyone passionately advocated for neoliberalism. Rather, neoliberalism's key shibboleths were depoliticised and treated as common sense. And because they were common sense, they were no longer worthy of critical interrogation. An event of huge significance, an event that could've launched us towards a better future, had once again passed us by.

The COVID-19 pandemic similarly could have propelled us towards something better. Beyond the foreground of lockdowns and nightly updates on the huge numbers of people we were told had lost their lives as a result of the disease, neoliberal governments discovered that, contrary to their own hitherto diligently maintained myths, there was in fact a magic money tree.[4,5] Governments produced their own sovereign currency to address an obvious need. In the wake of furlough schemes and the like, how could neoliberal administrations go back to the claim that they were financially constrained and unable to address the social crisis and the material needs of the people? After witnessing governments create hundreds of billions out of thin air, would the people continue to accept that social services were simply too expensive and demands for higher pay totally unrealistic? Would future governments be forced to admit that they did not depend upon tax revenues to fund public spending? Would they be forced to acknowledge that obsessing about the deficit was counterproductive and that states with their own sovereign currency are never compelled to borrow their own currency from financial markets?[6]

At the close of the pandemic, however, nothing much changed. Many western governments began to tentatively ditch their reliance on foreign production and complex supply chains, a process that overlapped with rising geopolitical tensions between America and its allies and the BRICS. But ultimately another opportunity to push history in a different direction was lost.[7] Of course, if we reach back further into history, we can quickly begin to construct a long list of events that could have changed things. While our experience often suggests the contrary, there are always opportunities to push history in a different direction.

The lesson is clear: if we really hope to take advantage of the next historic opportunity that comes our way, we need to begin to act politically now. We need to construct new political organisations from the ground up. We need to build solidarity and political commitment immediately. We need to engage in productive debate about how our new society will look and what it will mean for ordinary people. Such debate must be driven forwards by a commitment to avoid getting bogged down in fractious identitarian squabbles while maintaining our focus on those things that can materially improve the vast majority's quality of life. We must once again talk honestly and convincingly about the common good and how it can be planted at the very centre of public life. We also need to identify the core policies that will underpin our vision. We need to grow our political constituency and draw in representatives from across the cultural spectrum with our deep commitment to solidarity and common cause. We need to organise, steal ourselves against our powerful opponents and determinedly prepare for the next opportunity that arises as we tread our path into the future. To avoid the hard work of preparation is to accept that the future will not accord with our tastes and preferences. It will be shaped instead by those with the power and money to corrupt our politics and influence our cultures in the direction of a post-neoliberalism that resembles a reconfigured feudalism.

But what has all of this to do with nostalgia? I have tried to explain why working-class politics today seems irrevocably tied to the past. I have suggested that growing feelings of cultural and economic irrelevance are fully justified. Many among the working class see the present as disordered and unclear. And as we have seen, positive images of the future have been systematically erased, to the extent that huge numbers now feel a deep sense of foreboding about where we are going and what the future will mean for themselves and their children. Against such a background, it makes sense to look to the past to identify a modicum of consistency and positivity. The past for research participants seemed orderly, well-managed and logical. Their cultures equipped them with a sense of surety, familiarity and belonging. They knew, broadly, where they were going, who they were, what was expected of them and what they could expect of others. They felt more confident and generally free of the multifaceted challenges and anxiety they currently face. In the past, they could fully immerse themselves in the comforts of home, knowing without question that this was precisely where they were supposed to be.

It is now commonplace to chastise the nostalgic for his discomfort in the present and his supposed desire to go back to the past. However, very often such criticism omits any consideration of precisely why so many people today feel discomforted. Similarly, the suggestion that nostalgics want to go back to the past is often incorrect. As we have seen, rather than going back to the past, participants wanted to excavate the past in order to identify and transplant the past's good things into the present. These are positive and open sentiments that deserve to be taken seriously and appraised honestly. Nostalgia is incurable, and there is no logical reason why it should be considered the preserve of conservatives. We will all feel the pull of nostalgia at some point in our lives. To observe the past only as a space of irredeemable horror is counter-productive. Hope for the future finds a platform in our recollections of a positive past. Very often what drives us to act politically in the here and now isn't vague images of oppressed future generations but compelling narratives of how our forebears overcame oppression.

Rather than decry nostalgia as inherently conservative and potentially fascistic, it makes more sense for progressives to work with nostalgia and to build political programmes that seek to extend the achievements of the past. Nostalgia is a relativistic condition built on qualitative comparisons. Would it be so bad if we again sought to politically reintroduce some of the things that, during the social democratic age, compared better and were rather conventional entitlements? Would a commitment to full employment, incrementally improving standards of living, industrial innovation or a comprehensive welfare system represent regression? Would the return of the democratic state to the very centre of economic management inevitably lead to disaster? Would it really be so bad if we sought to cultivate a greater sense of community cohesion and a popular commitment to those things that are shared by all? Would we be needlessly sacrificing our hard-won freedoms if we began to tentatively nurture collective identities, return to collective projects and commit ourselves once again to the common good?

It is true that we do not possess a time machine. We cannot go back. We must be future facing and commit ourselves to ensuring that the future will be more habitable than is commonly assumed. However, we can thoroughly investigate the past to see what can be found there that might inspire innovative thinking about the future. We can seek to reintroduce a positive sense of continuity that can be tracked from the past, into the present and towards the future. We can also appraise and seek to realise the past's most appealing hopes and dreams for the future. Wouldn't attempting to realise the ambitious dreams of the past represent a bold plan for social and political renewal in the here and now? Our forebears did not dream of ubiquitous and multifaceted decline. They wanted future generations to retain fundamental values while expanding opportunities for all people to live more gratifying and contented lives.

Given the grave position we find ourselves in, we might also cautiously attempt to step into the future by revisiting the solid platforms that once existed in the past. These features of the past cannot be final destinations, but they can give us a reasonably firm foundation to momentarily pause as we consider how we might move progressively into the future. We cannot re-establish the contexts that aided the development of these solid platforms, but we can commit ourselves to honestly representing our present and seeking to build idealised versions of the past's achievements. How can we ensure that every individual has what they need to live a safe and satisfying life? How can we equip every citizen with the very best education and healthcare? How can we manage national economies in the interests of all?

People are entitled to their roots. They are entitled to feel attached to particular places and the cultures that shaped their development. The sanctimonious dismissal of such attachments erodes the continuity we need to imagine the functional societies of the future. To impugn any culture's particular past – and to suggest that anyone invested in that past is somehow aligned with or responsible for its worst elements – is a negation of the serious thinking we must devote to the task of determining how we can strategically move towards an idealised future from our present position. Nostalgia, we must remember, often contains an element of pain. It is not simply the tacky saccharine sentimentalism of the popular imagination. Nostalgia often hurts. It is shot through with yearning and inspired by a prevailing sense of absence. The pains of nostalgia can encourage popular critique of our inadequate present. It can push us to ask why positive things from the past have fallen away and why our present doesn't measure up to the past's positive expectations. This is not to say that nostalgia necessarily contains within it a kernel of emancipatory knowledge. Rather, it is to say that pain is constitutive of thought, and confronting pain can inspire the forms of knowledge we need to break free from the negativities of the present.[8] Pain distinguishes knowledge from mere calculation.[9] To assume that nostalgia is somehow antithetical to progress is to make a category error born of a refusal to accept the pain of critical thinking.

Our political ambitions are inevitably shaped by the past, whether we choose to recognise it or not. The past offers us a reasonably stable constellation of events, facts, narratives and ideas, whereas we can only gain a partial grip upon what is happening in the present. As we set ourselves to the task of putting together ambitious new blueprints for a future society we hope to bring to fruition, we are inevitably reliant upon the forms of knowledge bequeathed to us by the past.

I cannot say that a slight adjustment here and there will alter our trajectory and spare us from the horrors that appear to lie ahead. While it pains me to acknowledge it, all evidence indicates that our descent will continue. We know what must be changed but we cannot find the energy or the motivation to change it. It is true that great powers are aligned against us, but we must also acknowledge that we have been immobilised by cynicism. Things can be done, but there is no sign that they will be done. Those who contributed to this study cannot return to their lost community, and it seems highly unlikely that a new and nourishing community can form amid the ruins of the old. Faced with the suggestion that his work inspired a sense of hopelessness, Kafka is said to have opined that there is an infinite amount of hope in the world, but none for us. All that we have is each other, and unless we acknowledge that fact and rediscover our humanity, and unless we can shake off our cynicism and believe again, the path ahead seems clear.

ENDNOTES

INTRODUCTION: FALLING

(1) This is a short book, and unfortunately, there is no space to discuss the history of nostalgia or the various ways it has been used in cultural and political commentary. Instead, I encourage the reader to peruse Boym's *The Future of Nostalgia*; Routledge's *Nostalgia*; Davis's *Yearning for Yesterday*; Batcho's 'Nostalgia' and the various essays contained in Becker and Trigg's edited volume, *Routledge Handbook of Nostalgia*.

(2) Winlow and Hall's *Death of the Left*.

(3) The research discussed in this book was funded by The Leverhulme Trust (grant MRF - 2022 – 105), which kindly awarded me a Major Research Fellowship in 2022.

(4) Ethnographic research methods are discussed in detail by Treadwell, in his *Criminological Ethnography*. Hammersley and Atkinson's *Ethnography* is also a very useful resource.

(5) Lloyd's *The Harms of Work* offers an excellent ethnographic account of 'new working class' occupational cultures.

(6) Mitchell and Fazi's *Reclaiming the State* offers an excellent overview of these changes.

(7) Harvey's *A Brief History of Neoliberalism*, Slobodian's *Globalists* and Saad-Filho's *Growth and Change in Neoliberal Capitalism*.

(8) Winlow and Hall's *Violent Night* and *Rethinking Social Exclusion*. See also Lloyd's *Harms of Work* and Telford's *English Nationalism and Its Ghost Towns*.

(9) Ibid.; see Beynon and Hudson's *In the Shadow of the Mine*.

(10) Stedman-Jones' *Languages of Class*, Cannadine's *The Rise and Fall of Class in Britain*, and Hobsbawm's *Age of Extremes*.

(11) Ainsley's *The New Working Class*.

(12) Winlow and Hall, *Death of the Left*.

(13) Consider, for example, McBride and Smith's 'I feel like I'm in poverty. I don't do much outside of work other than survive'.

(14) Savage's *Social Class in the 21st Century*.

(15) Pakulski and Waters' *The Death of Class*.

(16) Evans' *A Nation of Shopkeepers*.

(17) Virlio, *Aesthetics of Disappearance*.

(18) The disappearance of collective identities has been discussed by theorists as diverse as Bauman (in, for example, *Liquid Modernity*), Habermas (*The Structural Transformation of the Public Sphere*), Balibar (*We, the People of Europe?*), Castells (*Rise of the Network Society*) and Touraine (*The Self-Production of Society*).

(19) On this issue, see Savage and Burrows' 'The coming crisis of empirical sociology'.

(20) The suggestion that we have reached the end of history, which begin to stir interest in the 90s, has prompted much useful theorising and critique. Fukuyama's *The End of History and the Last Man* got the ball rolling. Fukuyama offered an optimistic reading of the end of history, claiming that electoral democracy coupled with market capitalism represented the pinnacle of human civilisational evolution.

History would continue, but change would for the most part be contained within the system as it stood. More insightful contributions are summarised in Winlow et al.'s *Riots and Political Protest* and Hochuli et al.'s *The End of the End of History*.

(21) Winlow and Hall, *The Death of the Left*.

(22) Piketty's ubiquitous *Capital in the Twenty-First Century*.

(23) Winlow and Hall, *Death of the Left*.

(24) Lasch's *The Revolt of the Elites and the Betrayal of Democracy*, Frank's *What's the Matter With Kansas?* and Kotkin's *The New Class Conflict*.

(25) Winlow's *Badfellas*.

(26) Treadwell, op cit, Hammersley and Atkinson, op cit.

(27) On this issue, see Gray's *The New Leviathans*; Postman, *Amusing Ourselves to Death*.

(28) Winlow et al.'s *Rise of the Right*.

(29) Hall and Winlow's discussion of synecdoches in *Revitalizing Criminological Theory*.

(30) Hall and Winlow, 'Back to the future'. Guilluy, *Twilight of the Elites*.

(31) Wolf, *Capitalism Hits the Fan*; ONS, 'Personal and household finances in the UK'; Wilkinson and Pickett, *The Spirit Level*.

(32) Varoufakis, *Technofeudalism*; Kotkin, *The Coming of Neo-Feudalism*.

(33) Winlow and Winlow's 2022 article 'Is the neoliberal era coming to an end?' Brown's *In the Ruins of Neoliberalism*, Kotsko's *Neoliberalism's Demons*, Kotkin's *The Coming of Neo-Feudalism* and Wark's *Capital is Dead*.

(34) MacIntyre's seminal *After Virtue*.

(35) Here, I am referring to the work of John Rawls, and in particular his hugely influential *A Theory of Justice*. To be brief, Rawls emphasised the importance of equality, fairness and liberty and suggested these things were essential to the creation of a just society. However, Rawls' egalitarian liberalism was orientated far more

to negative liberty than is commonly suggested. In many respects, his work heralded the growth of progressive neoliberalism. See Forrester's excellent *In the Shadow of Justice*.

(36) Implied here is Ricoeur's work on the narrative character of history. For Riccoeur, human experience is made intelligible through the narrative form. Our understanding of time and our own experience are inevitably informed by narratives about history, change and continuity. See Ricoeur, *Time and Narrative*.

(37) See, for example, Fisher's *Capitalist Realism* and his *Ghosts of My Life*.

(38) Winlow and Hall, 'Shock and awe'.

(39) While this book is concerned with how nostalgia works, it does not offer a detailed exposition. Instead, see Boym, op cit; Routledge, op cit, and Lowenthal's *The Past Is a Foreign Country Revisited*.

(40) Wildschut et al., 'Nostalgia: Content, triggers, functions', Sedikides and Wildschut, 'Finding meaning in nostalgia' and Vess et al.'s 'Nostalgia as a resource for the self'.

(41) Bennett, 'Narrating family histories'.

(42) Freud's *Beyond the Pleasure Principle*.

(43) Winlow's 2015 article 'Trauma, guilt and the unconscious', and Winlow and Hall's 2009 article, 'Retaliate first'.

(44) This suggests a Lacanian reading of the role, function and practice of the superego. See, for example, Lacan's *Ecrits* or Žižek's *How to Read Lacan*.

CHAPTER 1: THE NEW POLITICS OF NOSTALGIA

(1) Matt's *Homesickness*.

(2) Batcho, 'Nostalgia'.

(3) Boym, op cit.

(4) Davis's excellent *Yearning for Yesterday*.

(5) A gap that drives us forwards in search of truths that might, we imagine, be used to finally fill the gap and establish wholeness. Here I am, in a roundabout way, referencing Lacan's model of the human subject. See Lacan, op cit.

(6) Ellison's *A Readers Guide to Proust's in Search of Lost Time*.

(7) In fact, Batcho claims that the valence of nostalgia has actually moved from 'bitter' to 'sweet' to 'bittersweet'. See Batcho 'Nostalgia'.

(8) Boym, op cit; Lowenthal, op cit; Anderson's *Imagined Communities*, Hobsbawm and Ranger's edited collection, *The Invention of Tradition* and Huyssen's *Present Pasts*.

(9) Anderson, op cit and Trouillot's *Silencing the Past*.

(10) Tulving's *Elements of Episodic Memory*, Conway's *Flashbulb Memories* and *Autobiographical Memories*, LeDoux's *The Emotional Brain*.

(11) Tulving op cit.

(12) Schacter, *Searching for Memory*.

(13) Tulving op cit; Loftus and Ketchum's *Witness for the Defense*.

(14) In *Memory, History, Forgetting*, Ricoeur claims subjective memories and ostensibly 'objective' histories are necessarily intertwined, especially in narrative forms. Ricoeur also addresses the manipulation and repression of memories. He calls for 'ethical memory practices' that centre upon the responsible and just responses to subjective memories and incorporates multiple perspectives in the recollection and narrativisation of history.

(15) Winlow and Hall, *Death of the Left*.

(16) See for example Nagel, *Kill All Normies*.

(17) Winlow and Hall, *Death of the Left*.

(18) Frank, op cit; Chesterton, op cit.

(19) See MacIntyre, op cit, and Winlow and Hall, *Death of the Left*, on emotivism.

(20) See, for example, McKenzie, 'The class politics of prejudice'.

(21) Embery, *Despised*; Goodhart, *The Road to Somewhere*.

(22) Mitchell, *Imperial Nostalgia*; Campanella and Dassu, *Anglo Nostalgia*.

(23) There is a huge literature on this topic, but Gilroy's *Postcolonial Melancholia* has been particularly influential.

(24) Liu's *Virtue Hoarders*.

(25) For example, Mitchell, op cit; Woods, op cit.

(26) Lasch, *The Culture of Narcissism*; Wilson, *Nostalgia*; Morton, *A People's History of England*; Hill's *A World Turned Upside Down*.

(27) Consider, for example, Bhambra, 'Brexit, Trump and "Methodological Whiteness"'; Koegler et al., 'The colonial remains of Brexit'; Beaumont, 'Brexit, Retrotopia and the perils of post-colonial delusions'; Campanella and Dassù, 'Brexit and nostalgia' and *Anglo Nostalgia*; Woods, *Rule, Nostalgia*; Mitchell, *Imperial Nostalgia*.

(28) Ibid. See also: El-Enany, *(B)Ordering Britain*; Judah, 'England's last gasp of empire'; Earle, 'The toxic nostalgia of Brexit'; Antonucci et al., 'The malaise of the squeezed middle'; Khalili, 'After Brexit'.

(29) Bhambra, op cit.

(30) Tudor, 'Ascriptions of migration'; Virdee and McGeever 'Racism, crisis, Brexit'.

(31) Among many others, see Konrad, 'Denial of racism and the Trump presidency'; Goldstein and Hall, 'Postelection surrealism and nostalgic racism in the hands of Donald Trump'; Bobo, 'Racism in Trump's America'; Inwood, 'White supremacy, white counter-revolutionary politics, and the rise of Donald Trump'.

(32) Frank, *People Without Power*; Eatwell and Goodwin, *National Populism*; Laclau, *On Populist Reason*.

(33) Mudde, *The Far Right Today*; Mondon and Winter, *Reactionary Democracy*.

(34) Winlow et al., *Rise of the Right*; Hochuli et al., *The End of the End of History*.

(35) Muller, *What Is Populism?* Mudde, *Populism*; Mounk, *The People vs Democracy*.

(36) See Mudde, *Populism*.

(37) Winlow et al., *Rise of the Right*.

(38) Guilluy, *Twilight of the Elites*.

(39) Fazi's 'Europe's insurgent right won't change anything' offers a very useful overview.

(40) Hall and Winlow, *Revitalizing Criminological Theory*.

(41) Goodhart, op cit.

(42) Embrey, op cit. Winlow et al., *Rise of the Right*.

(43) Ehrenreich and Ehrenreich, 'The new left and the professional managerial class'; Ehrenreich, *Fear of Falling*; Liu, *Virtue Hoarders*; Lind, *The New Class War*; Lasch, *The Culture of Narcissism*.

(44) MacIntyre, *After Virtue*.

(45) See, for example, Day's *SJWs Always Lie*.

(46) For example, Castells, *Networks of Outrage and Hope*; Tarrow, *Power in Movement*; Melucci, *Nomads of the Present*.

(47) This is one of the central fallacies that maintains neoliberalism's dominance. Of course, a currency issuing state cannot run out of the currency that it alone produces. Nor does it ever need to borrow the currency that it alone produces. On this issue, see Kelton, *The Deficit Myth*; Mitchell and Fazi, op cit; Tcherneva, *The Case for a Job Guarantee*.

(48) Kelton, op cit; Mitchell and Fazi, op cit; Tcherneva, op cit.

(49) Winlow et al., *Riots and Political Protest*; Žižek, *Did Somebody Say Totalitarianism?*

(50) Badiou, *The Meaning of Sarkozy*.
(51) Fraser, *The Old Is Dying and New Cannot Be Born*.
(52) Lacan, *Ecrits*; Žižek, *How to Read Lacan*; Winlow and Hall, *Rethinking Social Exclusion*.

CHAPTER 2: FEARING THE FUTURE

(1) Every effort has been made to maintain the anonymity of research participants. Each participant has been given a pseudonym, and their personal details altered.
(2) Some interviews were recorded but most were not. This is standard practice in ethnographic studies of this kind. Some participants preferred not to have their words recorded. Often recording was simply not practicable, given that most conversations were conducted outdoors, walking around participants' neighbourhoods. Research notes were taken as soon as it was possible to do so.

CHAPTER 3: LOST ROOTS

(1) Weil, 2023.
(2) For a thorough deconstruction of the argument about closed and open communities, see Winlow et al., *Rise of the Right*.
(3) Here I am adapting Mauss's analysis of gift giving. See Mauss, *The Gift*.
(4) Siedentop, *Inventing the Individual*.
(5) Arendt, *The Human Condition*.

CHAPTER 4: BEYOND MODERNISM

(1) My overall analysis of postmodernism is informed by the following books. Lyotard, op cit; Derrida, op cit; Jameson, *Postmodernism*; Eagleton, *The Illusions of Postmodernism*; Harvey, *The Condition of Postmodernity*; Royle, *Jacques Derrida*; Wade and Dundas, *Foucault in California*; Foucault's *The Birth of Biopolitics, The History of Sexuality, Discipline and Punish* and *The Foucault Reader*; Dean and Zamora's *The Last Man Takes LSD*; Zamora and Behrent, *Foucault and Neoliberalism*; Macey, *The Lives of Michel Foucault*.

(2) Lyotard's *The Postmodern Condition*, Derrida's *Writing and Difference*, and Butler's *The Psychic Life of Power* are good examples. I am aware that Butler is not usually categorised as a postmodernist, but I believe this is a mistake.

(3) Winlow and Hall, *Death of the Left*; Hall and Winlow 'Back to the future'; Pugh, *Speak for Britain*.

(4) Neatly captured by Holloway's *Change the World Without Taking Power*.

(5) Embrey, op cit; Winlow et al., *Rise of the Right*.

(6) A general belief explored in various ways by philosophical traditions as diverse as the stoics, the Epicureans, the Buddhists, the Platonists and the Kantians.

(7) See Slobodian, *Globalists*; Reinhoudt and Audier, *The Walter Lippmann Colloquium*.

(8) Fukuyama's *End of History and the Last Man*; Winlow et al.'s *Riots and Political Protest*; Žižek's *In Defense of Lost Causes*, and *Living in the End Times*; Hochuli et al.'s *The End of the End of History*.

(9) Fukuyama, 1992, offered a key point of departure. He did indeed suggest that historical change, properly understood, was unnecessary.

(10) Consider for example Žižek, *Living in the End Times*;
      Ranciere's *The Politics of Aesthetics* and *On the Shores
      of Politics*; Badiou, *The Rebirth of History*; Winlow
      et al., *Riots and Political Protest*.

(11) Brown's *Undoing the Demos*; Harvey's *A Brief
      History of Neoliberalism*; Saad-Filho's *Growth and
      Change in Neoliberal Capitalism*.

(12) Bauman's *Liquid Modernity*.

(13) Beck's *Risk Society*.

(14) Giddens' *Modernity and Self-Identity*.

(15) Here, I mean in the sense suggested by Mark Fisher
      in his *The Weird and the Eerie*. For Fisher, the eerie
      inspires a sense of unease and discomfort that seems
      to grow from unfamiliarity.

(16) Bauman's *Liquid Times*.

(17) See for example Lee and Solon's 'Trends in inter-
      generational income mobility'.

(18) On economic insecurity, see, for example, Lloyd's *The
      Harms of Work*, Ehrenreich's *Nickel and Dimed*,
      Standing's *The Precariat*, and Johnson's *Precariat*. On
      associated mental health problems, see Pickett and
      Wilkinson's *The Spirit Level*. On social disintegration,
      see Putnam's *Bowling Alone* and Bauman's *Liquid
      Modernity*. On political alienation, see Hochschild's
      Strangers in Their Own Land and Guilluy's *Twilight of
      the Elites*.

(19) Bauman's *Liquid Modernity*.

(20) See for example Steel et al.'s 'The global prevalence
      of common mental disorders: A systematic review
      and meta-analysis 1980–2013'.

(21) Winlow and Hall, 'What is an ethics committee?'
      Winlow, 'Beyond measure'.

(22) See for example Friedman's *The Lexus and the
      Oliver Tree*.

(23) Winlow and Hall 'Living for the weekend' and
      Violent Night.

(24) Beck, *Risk Society*.

(25) Lloyd, *Labour Markets and Identity on the Post-industrial Assembly Line.*

CHAPTER 5: PERMANENT REFORM

(1) Fraser, *The Old Is Dying and the New Cannot Be Born.*
(2) See for example Goodwin's *Values, Voice, Virtue.*
(3) Ibid.
(4) Winlow and Hall, *Death of the Left.*
(5) Žižek, passim.
(6) See Cederstrom and Fleming's *Dead Man Working.*
(7) See Crary's *24/7.*
(8) See Winlow and Hall's discussion of 'rainbow capitalism' in *Death of the Left.*
(9) See Cederstrom and Fleming, *Dead Man Working.*
(10) Ibid. See also Fisher's *Capitalist Realism.*
(11) Graeber, *Bullshit Jobs.*
(12) Implied here is Althusser's conceptualisation of interpellation. See his *Lenin and Philosophy.*
(13) See Lloyd's *The Harms of Work.*
(14) Ahmed, *On Being Included.*
(15) The connections between consumerism and social exclusion are discussed at length in Winlow and Hall's *Rethinking Social Exclusion.*
(16) See Lloyd's *The Harms of Work* and *Work and Identity on the Post-Industrial Assembly Line.*
(17) Winlow and Hall, *Violent Night.*
(18) The concept of deaptation was originally developed by Adrian Johnston. See his *Žižek's Ontology* and *Prolegomena to Any Future Materialism.* Also adapted and discussed at length by Winlow and Hall in *The Death of the Left* and by Hall and Winlow in *Revitalizing Criminological Theory.*
(19) Freud, *The Ego and Mechanisms of Defence.*
(20) Hall, *Theorizing Crime and Deviance.*

(21) McKenzie, *Getting By*; Savage, *Social Class in the 21 Century*.
(22) McKenzie, *Getting By*; Kotze, *The Myth of the Crime Decline*; Garthwaite, *Hunger Pains*.
(23) Wilson, *When Work Disappears*; Massey and Denton, *American Apartheid*; Lupton, *Poverty Street*; Burell, 'Lost in the churn?'

CHAPTER 6: INTIMATIONS OF POST-SOCIALITY

(1) Winlow and Hall, *Rethinking Social Exclusion*.
(2) Virilio, *Aesthetics of Disappearance*.
(3) Baudrillard, *Simulacra and Simulation* and *The Consumer Society*.
(4) Winlow, 'The uses of catastrophism'.
(5) Lloyd, 'Understanding the post-industrial assembly line'.
(6) McKenzie, 'Cloaking class'.
(7) Miijs and Savage, 'Meritocracy, elitism and inequality'.
(8) Winlow and Hall, *Death of the Left*.
(9) Washington, *The Case for Open Borders*; Jannesari, *Freedom of Movement*.
(10) Bartram, 'International migration, open borders debates, and happiness'.
(11) Rose, *The Intellectual Life of the British Working Classes*; Beynon and Hudson, op cit.
(12) See, for example, McIlroy et al., *The High Tide of British Trade Unionism*.
(13) See Marglin and Shor's *The Golden Age of Capitalism*.
(14) Heidegger, *Being and Time*.
(15) Ricoeur, *Memory, History, Forgetting*.

CHAPTER 7: TOWARDS A BETTER FUTURE

(1) Varoufakis, *Technofeudalism*; Kotkin, *The Coming of Neo-Feudalism*; Wark, *Capital is Dead*.
(2) The BRICS group of nations is so called because it was initially made up of Brazil, Russia, India, China and South Africa. See Cooper, 2016; Bond and Garcia, 2015.
(3) Žižek, *Event*; Badiou, *Being and Event*; Heidegger, *Contributions to Philosophy*.
(4) Briggs et al., *Lockdown*; Briggs et al. 'Working, living, and dying in Covid times'; Green and Fazi, *The Covid Consensus*.
(5) Winlow and Winlow, 'Is the neoliberal era coming to an end?' Hall, 'Neoliberalism and the opportunodemic'.
(6) Kelton, op cit; Mitchell and Fazi, op cit; Tcherneva, op cit.
(7) Hall, 'Neoliberalism and the opportunodemic'.
(8) Badiou, *Ethics*.
(9) Han, *The Palliative Society*.

BIBLIOGRAPHY

Ahmed, S. (2012) *On Being Included*, Durham, NC: Duke University Press.

Ainsley, C. (2018) *The New Working Class*, Bristol: Policy Press.

Althusser, L. (2006) *Lenin and Philosophy and Other Essays*, London: Aaker Books.

Anderson, B. (2016) *Imagined Communities*, London: Verso.

Antonucci, L., Horvath, L., Kutiyski, Y. and Krouwel, A. (2017) 'The malaise of the squeezed middle: Challenging the narrative of the 'left behind' Brexiter', *Competition & Change*, *21*, 3: 211–229.

Arendt, H. (2018) *The Human Condition*, Chicago, IL: University of Chicago Press.

Badiou, A. (2006) *Being and Event*, London: Continuum.

Badiou, A. (2010) *The Meaning of Sarkozy*, London: Verso.

Badiou, A. (2012) *The Rebirth of History*, London: Verso.

Badiou, A. (2013) *Ethics*, London: Verso.

Balibar, E. (2004) *We, the People of Europe?* Princeton, NJ: Princeton University Press.

Bauman, Z. (2000) *Liquid Modernity*, Oxford: Polity.

Bartram, D. (2010) 'International migration, open borders debates, and happiness', *International Studies Review*, 12, 3: 339–361.

Batcho, K. (2013) 'Nostalgia: The bittersweet history of a psychological concept', *History of Psychology*, 16, 3: 165–176.

Baudrillard, J. (1994) *Simulacra and Simulation*, Ann Arbor, MI: University of Michigan Press.

Baudrillard, J. (2016) *The Consumer Society*, London: Sage.

Beaumont, P. (2017) 'Brexit, Retrotopia and the perils of post-colonial delusions', *Global Affairs*, 3, 4–5: 379–390.

Beck, U. (1992) *Risk Society*, London: Sage.

Becker, T. and Trigg, D. (eds) (2004) *Routledge Handbook of Nostalgia*, London: Routledge.

Bennett, J. (2018) 'Narrating family histories: Negotiating identity and belonging through tropes of nostalgia and authenticity', *Current Sociology*, 66, 3: 449–465.

Beynon, H. and Hudson, R. (2021) *In the Shadow of the Mine*, London: Verso.

Bhambra, G. (2017) 'Brexit, Trump, and 'methodological whiteness': On the misrecognition of race and class', *British Journal of Sociology*, 68: S214–S232.

Bobo, L.D. (2017) 'Racism in Trump's America: Reflections on culture, sociology, and the 2016 US presidential election', *British Journal of Sociology*, 68: S85–S104.

Bond, P. and Garcia, A. (eds) (2015) *BRICS*, London: Pluto.

Boym, S. (2002) *The Future of Nostalgia*, London: Basic Books.

Briggs, D., Telford, L., Lloyd, A., Ellis, A. and Kotze, J. (2021a) *Lockdown*, London: Palgrave Macmillan.

Briggs, D., Ellis, A., Telford, L. and Lloyd, A. (2021b) 'Working, living, and dying in Covid times: Perspectives from frontline residential care workers in the UK', *Safer Communities*, *20*, 3: 208–222.

Brown, W. (2019) *In the Ruins of Neoliberalism*, New York, NY: Columbia University Press.

Burrell, K. (2016) 'Lost in the 'churn'? Locating neighbourliness in a transient neighbourhood', *Environment and Planning A*, *48*, 8: 1599–1616.

Butler, J. (1997) *The Psychic Life of Power*, Stanford, CA: Stanford University Press.

Campanella, E. and Dassù, M. (2019) 'Brexit and nostalgia', *Survival*, *61*, 3: 103–111.

Campanella, E. and Dassù, M. (2019) *Anglo Nostalgia*, Oxford: Oxford University Press.

Cannadine, D. (1998) *The Rise and Fall of Class in Britain*, New York, NY: Columbia University Press.

Castells, M. (2000) *The Rise of the Network Society*, Oxford: Wiley-Blackwell.

Castells, M. (2012) *Networks of Outrage and Hope*, Oxford: Polity.

Cederstrom, C. and Fleming, P. (2012) *Dead Man Working*, London: Zero.

Chesterton, G.K. (2022) *The GK Chesterton Collection*, London: Catholic Way Publishing.

Conway, M. (1985) *Autobiographical Memory*, Milton Keynes: Open University Press.

Conway, M. (1994) *Flashbulb Memories*, London: Psychology Press.

Cooper, A. (2016) *The BRICS*, Oxford: Oxford University Press.

Crary, J. (2014) *24/7*, London: Verso.

Davis, F. (2014) *Yearning for Yesterday*, London: The Free Press.

Day, V. (2015) *SJWs Always Lie*, London: Castalia House.

Dean, M. and Zamora, D. (2021) *The Last Man Takes LSD*, London: Verso.

Debord, G. (1994) *Society of the Spectacle*, London: Rebel Press.

Derrida, J. (2001) *Writing and Difference*, London: Routledge.

DiAngelo, R. (2019) *White Fragility*, London: Penguin.

Eagleton, T. (1992) *The Illusions of Postmodernism*, Oxford: Wiley-Blackwell.

Earle, S. (2017) 'The toxic nostalgia of Brexit', *The Atlantic*, 5/10/17. Accessible here: https://www.theatlantic.com/international/archive/2017/10/brexit-britain-may-johnson-eu/542079/

Eatwell, R. and Goodwin, M. (2018) *National Populism*, London: Pelican.

Ehrenreich, B. (2011) *Nickel and Dimed*, London: Granta.

Ehrenreich, B. (2020) *Fear of Falling*, New York, NY: Twelve.

Ehrenreich, B. and Ehrenreich, J. (1977) 'The new left and the professional managerial class', *Radical America*, *11*, 3: 7–25.

El-Enany, N. (2021) *(B)Ordering Britain*, Manchester: Manchester University Press.

Ellison, D. (2010) *A Readers' Guide to Proust's in Search of Lost Time*, Cambridge: Cambridge University Press.

Embrey, P (2020) *Despised*, Oxford: Polity.

Evans, D. (2023) *A Nation of Shopkeepers*, London: Repeater Books.

Fazi, T. (2024) 'Europe's insurgent right won't change anything', *Unherd*, 10/6/24.

Fisher, M. (2009) *Capitalist Realism*, London: Zero.

Fisher, M. (2022) *Ghosts of My Life*, London: Zero.

Fisher, M. (2016) *The Weird and the Eerie*, London: Repeater Books.

Forrester, K. (2021) *In the Shadow of Justice*, Princeton, NJ: Princeton University Press.

Foucault, M. (2010) *The Birth of Biopolitics*, London: Palgrave Macmillan.

Foucault, M. (2020) *Discipline and Punish*, London: Penguin.

Foucault, M. (2020) *The Foucault Reader*, London: Penguin.

Foucault, M. (2020) *The History of Sexuality*, London: Penguin.

Frank, T. (2005) *What's the Matter With Kansas?* New York, NY: Picador.

Frank, T. (2020) *People Without Power*, London: Scribe.

Fraser, N. (2019) *The Old Is Dying and the New Cannot Be Born*, London: Verso.

Freud, A. (1992) *The Ego and Mechanisms of Defence*, London: Routledge.

Freud, S. (2003) *Beyond the Pleasure Principle*, London: Penguin.

Friedman, T. (1999) *The Lexus and the Olive Tree*, New York, NY: Farrar.

Fukuyama, F. (1992) *The End of History and the Last Man*, London: Penguin.

Garthwaite, K. (2016) *Hunger Pains*, Bristol: Policy Press.

Giddens, A. (1991) *Modernity and Self-identity*, Oxford: Polity.

Gilroy, P. (2004) *Postcolonial Melancholia*, New York, NY: Columbia University Press.

Goodwin, M. (2023) *Values, Voice, Virtue*, London: Penguin.

Goldstein, D.M. and Hall, K. (2017) 'Postelection surrealism and nostalgic racism in the hands of Donald Trump', *HAU: Journal of Ethnographic Theory*, 7, 1: 397–406.

Goodhart, D. (2017) *The Road to Somewhere*, London: Penguin.

Graeber, D. (2019) *Bullshit Jobs*, London: Penguin.

Gray, J. (2023) *The New Leviathans*, London: Penguin.

Green, T. and Fazi, T. (2023) *The Covid Consensus*, London: Hurst.

Guilluy, C. (2020) *Twilight of the Elites*, Yale, CT: Yale University Press.

Habermas, J. (1992) *The Structural Transformation of the Public Sphere*, Oxford: Polity.

Hall, S. and Winlow, S. (2015) *Revitalizing Criminological Theory*, London: Routledge.

Hall, S. and Winlow, S. (2020) 'Back to the future: On the British liberal left's return to its origins', *International Journal of Media and Cultural Politics*, 16, 1: 65–73.

Hall, S. (2012) *Theorizing Crime and Deviance*, London: Sage.

Hall, S. (2023) 'Neoliberalism and the opportunodemic', *Extreme Anthropology*. doi:10.5617/jea.9940.

Hammersley, M. and Atkinson, P. (2019) *Ethnography*, London: Routledge.

Han, B-C. (2021) *The Palliative Society*, Oxford: Polity.

Harvey, D. (1991) *The Condition of Postmodernity*, Oxford: Wiley-Blackwell.

Harvey, D. (2007) *A Brief History of Neoliberalism*, Oxford: Oxford University Press.

Heidegger, M. (2012) *Contributions to Philosophy*, Bloomington, IN: Indiana University Press.

Heidegger, M. (2019) *Being and Time*, London: Martino Fine.

Hill, C. (1972) *A World Turned Upside Down*, London: Penguin.

Hobsbawm, E. (1995) *Age of Extremes*, London: Abacus.

Hobsbawm, E. and Ranger, T. (eds) (2012) *The Invention of Tradition*, Cambridge: Cambridge University Press.

Hochschild, A. (2018) *Strangers in Their Own Land*, New York, NY: The New Press.

Hochuli, A., Hoare, G. and Cunliffe, P. (2021) *The End of the End of History*, London: Zero Books.

Holloway, J. (2019) *Change the World Without Taking Power*, London: Pluto.

Huyssen, A. (2003) *Present Pasts*, Stanford, CA: Stanford University Press.

Inwood, J. (2019) 'White supremacy, white counter-revolutionary politics, and the rise of Donald Trump', *Environment and Planning C: Politics and Space*, 37, 4: 579–596.

Jameson, F. (1992) *Postmodernism: Or, the Cultural Logic of Late Capitalism*, London: Verso.

Jannesari, S. (2020) *Freedom of Movement*, London: Global Justice. Accessible here: https://www.globaljustice.org.uk/wp-content/uploads/2020/12/freedom_of_movement_booklet_1220_-_web.pdf

Johnson, M. (ed) (2015) *Precariat*, London: Routledge.

Johnston, A. (2008) *Žižek's Ontology*, Evanston, IL: Northwestern University Press.

Johnston, A. (2012) *Prolegomena to Any Future Materialism, Volume 1*, Evanston, IL: Northwestern University Press.

Judah, B. (2016) 'England's last gasp of empire', *New York Times*, 12/7/16. Accessible here: https://www.nytimes.com/2016/07/13/opinion/englands-last-gasp-of-empire.html

Kelton, S. (2021) *The Deficit Myth*, New York, NY: Murray.

Khalili, L. (2017) 'After Brexit: Reckoning with Britain's racism and xenophobia', *Poem*, 5, 2–3: 253–265.

Koegler, C., Malreddy, P. and Tronicke, M. (2020) 'The colonial remains of Brexit', *Journal of Postcolonial Writing*, 56, 5: 585–592.

Konrad, A. (2018) 'Denial of racism and the Trump presidency', *Equality, Diversity and Inclusion*, 37, 1: 14–30.

Kotkin, J. (2014) *The New Class Conflict*, New York, NY: Telos.

Kotkin, J. (2023) *The Coming of Neo-Feudalism*, New York, NY: Encounter Books.

Kotsko, A. (2018) *Neoliberalism's Demons*, Standford, CA: Stanford University Press.

Kotze, J. (2019) *The Myth of the Crime Decline*, London: Routledge.

Lacan, J. (2007) *Ecrits*, London: Norton.

Laclau, E. (2018) *On Populist Reason*, London: Verso.

Lasch, C. (1995) *Revolt of the Elites and the Betrayal of Democracy*, New York, NY: Norton.

Lasch, C. (2018) *The Culture of Narcissism*, New York, NY: Norton.

LeDoux, J. (1994) *The Emotional Brain*, New York, NY: Simon & Schuster.

Lee, C. and Solon, G. (2009) 'Trends in intergenerational income mobility', *The Review of Economics and Statistics*, 91, 4: 766–772.

Lind, M. (2020) *The New Class War*, New York, NY: Atlantic Books.

Liu, C. (2021) *Virtue Hoarders*, Minnesota, MN: University of Minnesota Press.

Lloyd, A. (2016) *Labour Markets and Identity on the Post-industrial Assembly Line*, London: Routledge.

Lloyd, A. (2016) 'Understanding the post-industrial assembly line: A critical appraisal of the call centre', *Sociology Compass*, *10*, 4: 284–293.

Lloyd, A. (2018) *The Harms of Work*, London: Routledge.

Loftus, E. and Ketchum, K. (1994) *Witness for the Defense*, London: St Martin's Press.

Lowenthal, D. (2015) *The Past is a Foreign Country Revisited*, Cambridge: Cambridge University Press.

Lukianoff, G. and Haidt, J. (2019) *The Coddling of the American Mind*, London: Penguin.

Lupton, R. (2003) *Poverty Street*, Bristol: Policy Press.

Lyotard, J-F. (1984) *The Postmodern Condition*, Manchester: Manchester University Press.

Macey, D. (2019) *The Lives of Michel Foucault*, London: Verso.

MacIntyre, A. (2013) *After Virtue*, London: Bloomsbury.

McBride, J. and Smith, A. (2022) ''I feel like I'm in poverty. I don't do much outside of work other than survive': In-work poverty and multiple employment in the UK', *Economic and Industrial Democracy*, *43*, 3: 1440–1466.

McIlroy, J., Fishman, N. and Campbell, A. (eds) (2007) *The High Tide of British Trade Unionism*, London: Merlin.

McKenzie, L. (2015) *Getting By*, Bristol: Policy Press.

Mckenzie, L.(2017) 'The class politics of prejudice: Brexit and the land of no-hope and glory', *British Journal of Sociology*, 68: S265–S280.

McKenzie, L. (2023) 'Cloaking class: Making the working class visible', in J. Gohrisch and G. Stedman (eds) *Affective Polarisation*, Bristol: Bristol University Press.

Marglin, S. and Schor, J. (eds) (1991) *The Golden Age of Capitalism*, Oxford: Oxford University Press.

Massey, D. and Denton, N. (1994) *American Apartheid*, Harvard, NJ: Harvard University Press.

Matt, S. (2014) *Homesickness*, Oxford: Oxford University Press.

Mauss, M. (2001) *The Gift*, London: Routledge.

Melucci, A. (1989) *Nomads of the Present*, London: Radius.

Mijs, J. and Savage, M. (2020) 'Meritocracy, elitism and inequality', *The Political Quarterly*, 91, 2: 397–404.

Mitchell, P. (2021) *Imperial Nostalgia*, Manchester: Manchester University Press.

Mitchell, W. and Fazi, T. (2017) *Reclaiming the State*, London: Pluto Press.

Mondon, A. and Winter, A. (2020) *Reactionary Democracy*, London: Verso.

Mounk, Y. (2019) *The People vs. Democracy*, Harvard, NJ: Harvard University Press.

Morton, A.L. (1996) *A People's History of England*, London: Lawrence & Wishart.

Mudde, C. (2017) *Populism*, Oxford: Oxford University Press.

Mudde, C. (2019) *The Far Right Today*, Oxford: Polity.

Muller, J-W. (2017) *What is Populism?* London: Penguin.

Murray, D. (2020) *The Madness of Crowds*, London: Bloomsbury.

Nagel, A. (2017) *Kill All Normies*, London: Zero.

ONS. (2015) 'Personal and household finances in the UK'. Accessible here: https://www.ons.gov.uk/peoplepopulationand community/personalandhouseholdfinances/incomeandwealth/ articles/personalandhouseholdfinancesintheuk/2015-02-12

Pakulski, J. and Waters, M. (1995) *The Death of Class*, London: Sage.

Piketty, T. (2017) *Capital in the Twenty-First Century*, Cambridge, MA: Harvard University Press.

Postman, N. (1985) *Amusing Ourselves to Death*, London: Methuen.

Pugh, M. (2011) *Speak for Britain!* London: Vintage.

Putnam, R. (2001) *Bowling Alone*, New York, NY: Simon & Schuster.

Ranciere, J. (2013) *The Politics of Aesthetics*, London: Bloomsbury.

Ranciere, J. (2021) *On the Shores of Politics*, London: Verso.

Rawls, J. (1999) *A Theory of Justice*, Havard, MA: Harvard University Press.

Reinhoudt, J. and Audier, S. (2017) *The Walter Lippmann Colloquium: The Birth of Neo-Liberalism*, London: Routledge.

Ricoeur, P. (1990) *Time and Narrative*, Chicago, IL: University of Chicago Press.

Ricoeur, P. (2006) *Memory, History, Forgetting*, Chicago, IL: University of Chicago Press.

Rose, J. (2021) *The Intellectual Life of the British Working Classes*, Yale, CT: Yale University Press.

Routledge, C. (2015) *Nostalgia*, London: Routledge.

Royal, N. (2003) *Jacques Derrida*, London: Routledge.

Saad-Filho, A. (2021) *Growth and Change in Neoliberal Capitalism*, Chicago, IL: Haymarket Books.

Savage, M. (2015) *Social Class in the 21st Century*, London: Pelican.

Savage, M and Burrows, R. (2007) 'The coming crisis of empirical sociology', *Sociology*, 41, 5: 885–899.

Schacter, D. (1996) *Searching for Memory*, New York, NY: Basic Books.

Sedikides, C. and Wildschut, T. (2018) 'Finding meaning in nostalgia', *Review of General Psychology*, 22, 1: 48–61.

Siedentop, L. (2015) *Inventing the Individual*, London: Penguin.

Slobodian, Q. (2018) *Globalists*, Cambridge, MA: Harvard University Press.

Standing, G. (2011) *The Precariat*, London: Bloomsbury.

Stedman-Jones, G. (2008) *Languages of Class*, Cambridge: Cambridge University Press.

Steel, Z., Marnane, C., Iranpour, C., Chey, T., Jackson, J.W., Patel, V. and Silove, D. (2014) 'The global prevalence of common mental disorders: A systematic review and meta-analysis 1980–2013', *International Journal of Epidemiology*, 43, 2: 476–493.

Tarrow, S. (2011) *Power in Movement*, Cambridge: Cambridge University Press.

Tcherneva, P. (2020) *The Case for a Job Guarantee*, Oxford: Polity.

Telford, L. (2022) *English Nationalism and Its Ghost Towns*, London: Routledge.

Touraine, A. (1977) *The Self-Production of Society*, Chicago, IL: University of Chicago Press.

Treadwell, J. (2019) *Criminological Ethnography*, London: Sage.

Trouillot, M-R. (2015) *Silencing the Past*, London: Beacon Press.

Tudor, A. (2023) 'Ascriptions of migration: Racism, migratism and Brexit', *European Journal of Cultural Studies*, 26, 2: 230–248.

Tulving, E. (2002) *Elements of Episodic Memory*, Oxford: Oxford University Press.

Varoufakis, Y. (2024) *Technofeudalism*, London: Vintage.

Vess, M., Arndt, J., Routledge, C., Sedikides, C. and Wildschut, T. (2012) 'Nostalgia as a resource for the self', *Self and Identity*, 11, 3: 273–284.

Virdee, S. and McGeever, B. (2020) 'Racism, crisis, brexit', in S. Gupta and S. Virdee (eds) *Race and Crisis*, London: Routledge.

Virilio, P. (2009) *Aesthetics of Disappearance*, London: Semiotext.

Wade, S. and Dundas, H. (2021) *Foucault in California*, London: Heyday.

Wark, M. (2021) *Capital is Dead*, London: Verso.

Washington, J. (2024) *The Case for Open Borders*, London: Haymarket.

Weil, S. (2023) *The Need for Roots*, London: Penguin.

Wildschut, T., Sedikides, C., Arndt, J. and Routledge, C. (2006) 'Nostalgia: Content, triggers, functions', *Journal of Personality and Social Psychology*, *91*, 5: 975–993.

Wilkinson, R. and Pickett, K. (2010) *The Spirit Level*, London: Penguin.

Wilson, J. (2005) *Nostalgia*, Lewisburg, PA: Bucknell University Press.

Wilson, W. J. (1996) *When Work Disappears*, New York, NY: Knopf.

Winlow, S. (2001) *Badfellas: Crime, Tradition and New Masculinities*, Oxford: Berg.

Winlow, S. (2015), 'Trauma, guilt and the unconscious: Some theoretical notes on violent subjectivity', *Sociological Review*, *62*, Supplement S2: 32–49.

Winlow, S. (2017), 'The uses of catastrophism', in R. Atkinson, L. McKenzie and S. Winlow (eds) *Building Better Societies*, Bristol: Policy Press.

Winlow, S. (2022), 'Beyond measure: On the marketization of British Universities, and the domestication of academic criminology', *Critical Criminology*, *30*: 479–49.

Winlow, S. and Hall, S. (2006) *Violent Night: Urban Leisure and Contemporary Culture*, Oxford: Berg.

Winlow, S. and Hall, S. (2009) 'Living for the weekend: Youth identities in northeast England', *Ethnography*, *10*, 1: 91–113.

Winlow, S. and Hall, S. (2009), 'Retaliate first: Memory, humiliation and male violence', *Crime, Media, Culture*, *5*, 3: 285–304.

Winlow, S. and Hall, S. (2012), 'What is an 'Ethics Committee'? Academic governance in an epoch of belief and incredulity', *British Journal of Criminology*, *52*, 2: 400–441.

Winlow, S. and Hall, S. (2012) *Rethinking Social Exclusion: The End of the Social?* London: Sage.

Winlow, S. and Hall, S. (2019), 'Shock and awe: On progressive minimalism and retreatism, and the new ultra-realism', *Critical Criminology*, *27*: 21–36.

Winlow, S., Hall, S., Treadwell, J. and Briggs, D. (2015) *Riots and Political Protest: Notes from the Post-Political Present*, London: Routledge.

Winlow, S., Hall, S. and Treadwell, J. (2017) *Rise of the Right: English Nationalism and Working-Class Politics*, Bristol: Policy Press.

Winlow, S. and Hall, S. (2022) *Death of the Left: Why We Must Begin From the Beginning Again*, Bristol: Policy Press.

Winlow, S. and Winlow, E. (2022), 'Is the neoliberal era coming to an end? Ideology, history and macroeconomic change in the shadow of COVID 19', *Journal of Contemporary Crime, Harm, and Ethics*, 2, 1: 1 – 23.

Wolf, R. (2010) *Capitalism Hits the Fan*, London: Interlink.

Woods, H. (2022) *Rule, Nostalgia*, London: Penguin.

Zamora, D. and Behrent, M. (eds) (2016) *Foucault and Neoliberalism*, Oxford: Polity.

Žižek, S. (2006) *How to Read Lacan*, London: Granta.

Žižek, S. (2008) *In Defense of Lost Causes*, London: Verso.

Žižek, S. (2010) *Living in the End Times*, London: Verso.

Žižek, S. (2011) *Did Somebody Say Totalitarianism?* London: Verso.

Žižek, S. (2014) *Event*, London: Penguin.

www.ingramcontent.com/pod-product-compliance
Lightning Source LLC
Chambersburg PA
CBHW050650270326
41927CB00012B/2957